PART ONE

WHITE WINE.

THEIR DETRACTORS WRITE OFF THE LIGHT, DRY WHITES AS BORING AND FLAVOURLESS, BUT THOSE IN THE KNOW POINT TO SOME OF THESE WINES AS THE MOST ELEGANT AND REFRESHING AROUND. A few are even complex and satisfying, although you will unfortunately encounter some flavourless, mediocre bottles along the way. A premium light, dry white has a lovely crispness, subtle fruit flavours and, perhaps, a pretty, aromatic hint of blossom. It may be delicate, but a good light white wakes up the palate, makes the mouth water and whets the appetite like no other table wine. It also washes down a range of summery dishes wonderfully well – leafy salads, white fish and pasta in creamy sauces. And the greatest quality is how easygoing and enjoyable it is – unlike, say, a heavily oaked Chardonnay that may effortlessly win a wine competition, but which you don't want to drink in any great quantity. Light, dry whites should always be highly drinkable and moreish.

So, how can you avoid those dull bottles? Cool climates count for a lot; pick a wine from a place where the grapes retain pure fruit flavours and that essential 'zing' of acidity. Warm climates just don't do the same trick. Go for the better grape varieties – Riesling, Verdicchio and Grüner Veltliner – which are more likely to make wine with flavour, rather than second-rate ones – Müller-Thurgau and Trebbiano – which tend to produce uninspiring, bland whites. Riesling, in particular, is in a league of its own. With all light, dry whites, try to track down a winemaker who uses low-yielding vines (for more concentration in the grapes) rather than fertile, high-cropping ones. Not much on the label will tell you this, but some of the tips on the next few pages will point you towards the right wines. Trading up a notch from the basic, rustic whites, churned out as cheap-and-cheerful gluggers, will help you avoid the sort of wine that's a yawn and instead give you a crisp, zesty wake-up call to the senses!

APPEARANCE

Pale-straw colour, sometimes with light-green hints. Not golden-yellow like richer or sweeter white wines.

TEXTURE

Relatively thin, light, watery, neither viscous nor weighty.

AROMA

Good examples smell of fresh, tangy citrus fruit: lemons, limes, grapefruit, and crunchy green apples. Some have a floral note, others a hint of almond. Second-rate, dull examples have little aroma or smell grubby.

FLAVOUR

Should have a refreshing, succulent streak of acidity. Again, look out for those citrus fruits and freshly chopped apples. A clean, crisp, mineral finish.

RIESLING

NATURALLY LIGHT AND ELEGANT

The Riesling grape is refreshing in more ways than one. Of course, as anyone who has tried true Riesling will know, it is one of the world's greatest aperitifs – naturally light and elegant yet racy, with mouth-watering citrus and apple fruit and quite a crisp finish. So it's refreshing in the most obvious sense of the word. But Riesling is also refreshing in that it makes a welcome change from all the Chardonnay and Sauvignon Blanc that fills our shop shelves.

It is a quite different style of wine, as will become clear below. But why the need to say 'true' Riesling? That's because this poor grape gets blamed – unfairly – for much of the light, white dross out there. Many have the wrong idea about Riesling; they think it's the variety behind the blandest, least memorable light whites, when cheaper, less well-known grapes are usually responsible. If I handed you a glass of fine Riesling, you'd probably be amazed at how much delicious flavour there is – and how tangy, vivacious and delightfully fresh the wine seems. So, don't confuse Riesling with lesser wines. It's consistently delightful, and remarkably long-lived to boot. In fact, for many serious wine buffs, this is the greatest white grape of all.

GERMANY

Fine German Riesling is a very different creature from cheap and nasty German plonk, so if you've never tried it, give it a go. It's no surprise that this type of wine is often described as one of the trade's best kept secrets – plenty of aficionados out there love it despite its untrendy image! A cool climate produces wines that are never over-the-top – restraint, subtlety and elegance are the watchwords. Alcohol levels remain naturally low – seven or eight percent is not unusual, and nine or ten percent is quite common (compared to twelve to fourteen percent in many other table wines).

That said, the style does vary from bottle to bottle – too much so at times, as it can be hard to know exactly what type of Riesling you are getting by looking at the label. Here are some tips: the Mosel region makes the prettiest, most delicate examples, with a spring-like, apple-blossom scent, although there is still a spine-tingling acidity in many; the Rheingau makes more intense, fuller-bodied versions, while the Pfalz is a progressive region, turning out more juicy, fruity, modern styles.

The main problem is picking a level of sweetness you enjoy – whether it's bone-dry and bracing, medium with a dab of honeyed weight or luscious and sticky. Germany makes Riesling at all levels of sweetness, but the most densely written Gothic labels are not easy to read. Incidentally, this is one reason fine German wines have gone out of fashion – consumers find the words on, say, an Australian bottle much easier to follow.

For the record: the word *trocken* on a label means dry, while *halbtrocken* means semi-dry. Meanwhile, the top quality category of Riesling (these bottles say *Qualitätswein mit Prädikat* or QmP on the label), ones made according to certain strict rules and regulations, are divided into six categories according to the ripeness of the grapes used, and this (rather roughly) corresponds to their dryness/sweetness levels. *Kabinett* indicates dry, *Spätlese* is a riper, often off-dry style, and *Auslese*, *Beerenauslese*, *Trockenbeerenauslese* and *Eiswein* follow next in order of increasing sweetness. Then there are certain wines which have been made from fruit grown in the best sites – *Erstes Gewächs*, or 'first growth'. These specific vineyard areas are named on the label.

Complicated? Yes. German Riesling does takes a bit of getting to know. But it is worth it. Once you have convinced yourself, try these tantalising, lip-smacking whites on your friends; if they are dubious, then let them taste it before telling them it's a German wine. I bet most of them will love it and will be converted to the joys of Riesling.

On the other hand, there are some small signs now that German Riesling is set to become a bit more fashionable. Most people have got over their obsession with chunky, oaky southern hemisphere whites and recognise that there are other, more subtle, white wines out there. The prices are also fair – very fair, in fact – and a good Riesling is also wonderfully food-friendly in a way that a monster Californian Chardonnay will never be.

Finally, don't miss the chance to try an older German Riesling. If it is stored correctly, it will lose its spiky, acid edge, softening and mellowing, and taking on a more honeyed, toffee-apple appeal. Then there's

something else about older Riesling – it acquires a distinct whiff of lanolin and petrol. That sounds horrible, but it isn't; instead, it gives a lovely warm, mellow richness to the older wines. Give them a go – you have to try aged Riesling for yourself to see just what I mean. Once you've started drinking German Riesling, you can start to become an expert by comparing wines from particular vineyard sites, as they give a fascinating insight into the effects of different soils and micro-climates.

FRANCE

The second-best place in the world for producing Riesling is Alsace in eastern France. This region is on the French border with Germany and has at several times during its history been part of Germany, so it's hardly surprising that Riesling is an important grape here. Wines that come from Alsace can even look confusingly Germanic, with a tall bottle shape, Germanic names and sometimes Gothic script on the label, so be careful to distinguish the two – they are quite different in taste. Alsace Rieslings have a richer, more full-bodied character, and the alcohol levels are usually higher – back up to normal table-wine levels rather than unusually low. They should still have that tell-tale streak of fresh acidity, though, and the best examples should age well.

Look out for the prestigious *grand cru* wines – over fifty of the best vineyard sites (*grands crus*, named on the label) are meant to indicate the best fruit in the region. Some are superb, but others just don't quite deserve the honour and extra cost that a *grand cru* wine can fetch. Match them with richer food than the German Rieslings, such as a cheese-and-onion tart or fish in creamy sauces. Good producers are: Trimbach, Zind-Humbrecht and, for good value, Turckheim.

REST OF EUROPE

Austria makes some impressive dry Riesling, with tart, intense lemon fruit and a bracing mineral quality. Some have a weighty, full texture (expect thirteen percent alcohol – much higher than in Germany) and should age well. Try one made near to Vienna or from the region of Styria or, best of all, from the Wachau region in Lower Austria, where the cool climate and well-drained soils help create some brilliant wines. Bründlmayer, Hirtzberger, FX Pichler are names to look out for. A few rather lean, but refreshing Rieslings are made in northern Italy, mostly in the cool northeast of the country. Go for wines produced in the Trentino or Alto-Adige regions.

REST OF THE WORLD

Australian Riesling is a 'must-try' – you will see a completely different side to the grape. Sure, the crisp acidity is still there, and that citrus fruit is to the fore, but this is a riper type of Riesling, a sun-kissed wine, with juicy lime the most obvious characteristic. If it is given enough time (five years or more), that crisp edge softens and toasty, honeyed layers begin to appear, while that freshly chopped fruit becomes more like lime marmalade... Delicious! A suggestion of petrol or kerosene can also be identified in a properly matured example.

Clare Valley and Eden Valley (both in the south) and Tasmania are key regions for producing good quality Australian Riesling. Interestingly, before the boom in Chardonnay plantings, Riesling was the most widely planted white grape Down Under, and now winemakers seem to have revived their interest, so look out for a growing number appearing on the shelves. Good labels to try include: Mount Langi Ghiran, Tim Adams and Henschke, and at the cheaper end, even the Jacob's Creek Riesling is a corker!

While we're in the Antipodes, don't miss out on New Zealand Riesling. It's similar to the Australian style, bursting with citrus fruit, but has a pithier, more mineral-dry edge. The South Island wine regions make the best – especially Marlborough, Central Otago and Waipara/Canterbury. Felton Road, Giesen, Villa Maria and Hunter's all produce fine examples.

Canada is another country excelling with dry Riesling – it's a pity the wines are not more widely available. The sweet Rieslings of Canada are more renowned but if you come across a dry one, snap it up. In the United States, most wine is sourced from California, but not Riesling. Although a very few decent West Coast examples do exist (from high-altitude, cool sites), better Riesling has come out of Washington State, Oregon and the Finger Lakes in New York State, where winemakers concentrated on this variety while the Californians went mad for Chardonnay.

SAUVIGNON BLANC

LIGHT AND LEAN STYLES

Sauvignon Blanc can often be very fruity and pungent, and because of this the grape is dealt with in more detail in the next chapter, 'Fruity, Spicy Whites' (see pages 50–55). Nonetheless, light, lean Sauvignons do exist in the form of Sancerre and Pouilly-Fumé and other wines from the cool Loire Valley.

FRANCE

Sancerre is perhaps the most famous appellation for Sauvignon Blanc – it produces extremely attractive, bone-dry, lemony wines, while nearby Pouilly-Fumé wines are known for their mineral, slightly smoky note (think of a spark of gun-flint; the whiff of smoke from a fired pistol). The best vineyards where these wines are produced have chalk over clay soils, with some patches of flint, the latter known as silex soils and said to produce the most long-lived wines. Top Sancerre and Pouilly-Fumé are, for many, the most elegant and hauntingly beautiful Sauvignons of all, and from a fine winemaker such as Cotat Frères, De Ladoucette or Didier Dagueneau, so they are, but many inferior wines exist, too, and prices are not low. Better-value premium Sauvignon sometimes comes from less well-known parts of the Loire – Quincy, Reuilly and Menetou-Salon, while for everyday quaffing, Sauvignon de Touraine and Vin de Pays du Jardin de la France Sauvignon Blanc (Loire 'country wines' made from this grape) can

hardly be bettered for simple, zesty refreshment at very reasonable prices. Further southwest, around the wider Bordeaux area, plenty of simple quaffing wines made from Sauvignon alone or Sauvignon and Sémillon are produced. The great oaked Bordeaux whites have no place in this section as they are certainly not light, but basic Bordeaux Blanc and whites from Bergerac and Entre-Deux-Mers provide a vast sea of Sauvignon of variable quality. A superior example is lemony and dry with a distinct note of freshly chopped grass. It would be wrong to generalise hugely about so much wine, but while most are palatable, south west Sauvignon doesn't tend to have the snappy, pure Sauvignon character that the Loire provides.

REST OF EUROPE

Austria is a source of fine Sauvignon, bracingly crisp and mouth-watering, the best of which is made in the Styria region to the south. Some have startlingly high acidity, guaranteed to wake-up tired taste buds, although toned-down, less nervy wines, even some rich, oak-aged ones, have started to emerge more recently. Northern Italy is another important destination for the Sauvignon lover, the cool, high-altitude vineyards of the Friuli-Venezia-Guilia and Trentino-Alto Adige regions making simple, lean, racy Sauvignons that are refreshing but no more complex than that.

REST OF WORLD

Some lighter, crisper styles of Sauvignon are made in the coolest New World vineyards, such as Tasmania, Waipara/Canterbury in New Zealand, Casablanca Valley in Chile and Elgin in South Africa. These wines major on tangy citrus fruit rather than the richer, fruiter styles more generally seen in the New World (see pages 50-55).

OTHER LIGHT, DRY WHITES

PLENTY MORE TO PICK FROM

2001
PINOT GRIGIO
DELLEVENEZIE
INDICAZIONE GEOGRAFICA TIPICA

CONNUBIO

WELSCHRIESLING/ LASKI RIZLING

Don't make the mistake of thinking that all whites with Riesling/Rizling on the bottle are true Riesling. Welschriesling, aka Laski Rizling, has absolutely nothing to do with our fine German friend, and it makes much less exciting light, dry whites. These wines tend to be bland with a lower acidity (i.e. less refreshing) and they certainly don't age well, turning flat and dull within just a matter of months. A few palatable examples of Welschriesling come from Austria, but generally, this grape should be avoided in favour of real Riesling.

MUSCADET/MELON DE BOURGOGNE

Taste a poor Muscadet and you will probably start to wonder what all the fuss is about – it's simple, perhaps a little too tart, and frankly rather boring. Certainly nothing to write home about. The product of the area around Nantes in France's Loire Valley, this wine is a little overrated, although there are signs of a revival. But, still, there is a big jump in quality from basic Muscadet to the finest wines.

Premium Muscadet is aged on its yeast sediment (lees), which gives it a creamier edge, perhaps with a hint of fresh bread or even yoghurt, and in youth, a fresh prickle on the tongue of carbon dioxide gas. Quality is on the up in the Loire Valley and there are much better wines around now than there were only a decade ago. Look out for the words *sur lie* on a label. This will indicate a wine that has been bottled on the lees. Try to avoid the bargain basement examples here.

Melon de Bourgogne, by the way, is the real name for the grape that makes Muscadet. Good Muscadet is a decent wine for washing down seafood, especially oysters.

MÜLLER-THURGAU

This is the main grape behind many cheap, once-popular German whites that are now less fashionable: Hock, Liebfraumilch, Niersteiner and Piesporter. There's nothing inherently wrong with a clean, fresh example, but don't expect much. Müller-Thurgau has very little character compared with Riesling (which, ironically, is one of its parents – this is a modern cross between Riesling and a more obscure grape variety). It has hardly any fragrance or complexity, but growers love it as the vines flourish easily and produce loads of fruit. Plantings are in decline now, but it is still widely planted in Germany and it's a similar story in New Zealand: Müller-Thurgau was a major player here until recently, when other grapes started to prove more popular. Drinkers had simply discovered wines with better flavours and it fell from grace. It is just about possible to make a half-decent Müller-Thurgau, and a few producers in New Zealand and Germany do so (as well as one or two in Italy and, believe it or not, England) but it takes a lot of care in the vineyard, and very low yields to make interesting wine.

PINOT GRIGIO AND OTHER ITALIAN WHITES

We're talking Pinot Grigio, Frascati, Soave and Orvieto here – a quartet of Italian whites that all taste light, clean, crisp and fresh. That's the idea, anyway. In reality there are too many oxidised and disappointing examples of all four around. The bland and characterless Trebbiano grape plays a major part in the production of Frascati, Soave and Orvieto. Cheap examples of these wines use mainly Trebbiano, while better bottles use higher proportions of a tastier grape such as Garganega in Soave. Pinot Grigio is the same as France's Pinot Gris grape, which makes rich and opulent wines in

Alsace, but light, lemony, sometimes spritzy whites in Italy. Try to find bottles that are fresh into the shop rather than those which have been hanging around collecting dust, as Pinot Grigio doesn't last well. And go for reputable producers – top Soave, say, from a fastidious winemaker, has bags more flavour than dirt-cheap, mass-produced Soave.

Frascati, Soave and Orvieto come from Lazio, Verona and Umbria, respectively. At their best, Frascati and Orvieto taste of fresh lemons with a hint of floral violet aroma. Soave can be more interesting, with creamier depths and a richer note of almond oil from a top producer (Pieropan is one name to look out for). Although these wines are more easily available, lesser-known whites from the central Marches region made from a grape called Verdicchio (this appears on the label) are more exciting: still fresh and snappy, but with a greater depth of limey flavour.

DRY MUSCAT

The Muscat family of related grape varieties is widespread, and many of the wines produced by its scions are sweet. But aromatic, dry Muscat is well worth a taste if you come across it. This is the only white wine that truly tastes of grapes above any other fruit – crunchy green grapes fresh from the fridge in the case of crisp, young, cold dry Muscat. As such it is a pretty, summery wine – perfect for hot days sitting in the garden, should any come our way! Dry Muscat is a speciality of Alsace in eastern France (try it with fresh asparagus) and there are a few great-value examples from Italy, Austria, Germany (where it is called Muskateller), and also Australia.

UGNI BLANC AND COLOMBARD

Colombard's roots are firmly in the Cognac region of France where it has been a mainstay of brandy production for centuries. One of the reasons it works so well in brandy is that the base wine it produces is neutral in character, so there you go – it makes pretty boring table wine. In the right hands, though, it can be fairly crisp and quaffable and it does have a light, floral edge. It is blended with Ugni Blanc to make the snappy, refreshing country wine Vin de Pays des Côtes de Gascogne and is also used for basic but palatable crisp whites in South Africa. Ugni Blanc is called Trebbiano in Italy (where it plays a major role in the Italian whites described above). It does not have enough natural character to create interesting wine.

GRÜNER VELTLINER

Austria's very own white grape makes distinctive wines with a clear note of white pepper twisted over racy citrus fruit. Not yet well-known overseas, Grüner Veltliner can produce strikingly good wines, wonderfully dry and lean yet full of flavour, and the best will even taste weighty and rich in texture, if tangy and succulent, and will age well for a couple of years. One to try if you fancy a change! Bründlmayer and Freie Weingärtner Wachau (FWW) are labels to sample.

ALIGOTÉ

Burgundy is famous for its world-beating Chardonnays (see pages 81–84), but another white grape also grows there. Aligoté is not nearly as important as Chardonnay in the region, and it doesn't create anything like such impressive wine, but as with many of the grapes described above, it makes a refreshing change. It generally produces wines that are tart and light, sometimes with a very slight spritz of gas, but ripe examples from a warm vintage can be a little creamier and fuller. Traditionally, this is the base wine for 'kir' – add a splash of crème de cassis (from Dijon if you want to be loyal to Burgundy!) to a glass of young, cold Aligoté for a wonderful summer aperitif.

STORING AND SERVING

SERVE THE LIGHT, DRY WHITES NICE AND COLD TO EMPHASISE THEIR REFRESHING, MOUTH-WATERING TANGINESS. Store in the fridge for at least an hour or two before serving, then keep the bottle cool by putting it on ice or back in the fridge. Serve in medium-sized white wine glasses (nothing too small or else you won't get the full benefits of those delicate aromas as you swirl the glass). A long-stemmed, elegant, plain glass is perfect for holding and looking at your wine. Very light, simple, dry whites need drinking up almost as soon as you buy them, as they will lose their fragile fragrance and fruit flavour very quickly. Good, crisp Sauvignon should stand up better for a few months, while a fine Riesling is surprisingly long-lived. Drink it up when young sometimes, but do try an older Riesling once in a while for a taste of honeyed apple, yet a dry finish, and even that famous hint of petrol on the aroma.

MAKING THE DIFFERENCE

LIGHT, DRY WHITES HAVE IMPROVED NO END IN QUALITY OVER THE PAST FIFTEEN YEARS OR SO; PUT SIMPLY, THEY ARE MORE RELIABLY FRESH, CLEAN AND CRISP THAN THEY USED TO BE. This is due partly to more sensitive handling of the grapes between picking and fermenting, so that subtle flavours are not lost, and partly to the use of low, controlled temperatures during fermentation. The wine is now usually fermented in stainless-steel tanks – much more hygienic than old-fashioned concrete vats. Indeed, hygiene is considered very important at wineries these days, and light, dry whites have benefitted hugely. There are still some oxidised, faded or plain grubby whites around, but fewer than ever before.

MATCHING LIGHT, DRY WHITES WITH FOOD

SUCCESSFUL FOOD-AND-WINE MATCHING IS ALL ABOUT BALANCING LIKE WITH LIKE OR, IN THIS CASE, LIGHT WITH LIGHT! Never match a tart, lean, dry white with very rich food or any form of red meat. Instead, these wines go well with crisp dishes such as tomato salad, grilled peppers and asparagus, and even stand up reasonably well to fruity or acidic salad dressings. They are great with white fish dishes, simple fresh seafood and, more surprisingly, they are good at washing down mild chicken and vegetable curries. Sauvignon Blanc is a wow with goat's cheese.

FIRST TASTE

■ If a light, dry white isn't refreshing, there's something seriously wrong with it! These wines are meant to be MOUTH-WATERING, PALATE-CLEANSING, TANGY AND CRISP, so reject any examples that taste flat and flabby – i.e.lacking in zesty fruit and acidity. They may be corked or just badly made, but they won't reach the spot!

■ TRY TO SAVOUR THE DELICATE AROMAS AND FLAVOURS. Even the most committed fan of full-on, ultra-fruity Chardonnay can learn to love their elegance and subtlety, if they take time to stop and notice the more restrained but often complex layers of scent and taste.

■ If you are bored with dull, light whites, TRY WINES MADE FROM PREMIUM GRAPE VARIETIES only and from top spots – Riesling from the Mosel in Germany, say, or Sauvignon Blanc from Sancerre in the Loire Valley. Avoid the cheapest wines from less interesting grapes.

■ Be aware that SOME LIGHT WHITES ARE MUCH DRIER THAN OTHERS. Some are medium and will taste distinctly sweet to those used to bracing, bone-dry whites. That doesn't necessarily mean they are poor quality, but they may not be to your taste. If you aren't sure what's in your bottle, TRY BEFORE YOU BUY.

BUYER'S GUIDE

■ Unless you are buying mature Riesling, aim to buy young, light whites. Bag the most recent vintage you can, and if the wine is non-vintage, check with the shop that it is a recent shipment. NEVER BUY LIGHT WHITES THAT HAVE BEEN SITTING AROUND TOO LONG, especially if they look dusty or the liquid has turned darker yellow.

■ SOME INEXPENSIVE FRENCH WINES IN THIS STYLE PROVIDE GOOD VALUE – young Vin de Pays des Côtes de Gascogne, or Sauvignon de Touraine, is heartwarmingly cheap, yet reliably fresh and appealing. Don't expect anything too exciting, though.

■ Further up the quality ladder, RIESLING CAN BE REMARKABLY CHEAP – partly as it has been out of fashion for a long time (except among wine aficionados, who have always loved it). Germany in particular offers some seriously good, light, white Riesling for little outlay.

■ THE CRISPEST, TANGIEST, MOST TANTALISINGLY SUBTLE, LIGHT WHITES COME FROM COOLER CLIMATES. Wines made in this style from hotter areas tend to taste bigger, riper and sometimes even oily – fine if you like that kind of thing, but not truly very 'light' and sometimes lacking finesse and subtlety.

MOVING ON

■ Germany and Austria make some of the best examples of light, dry whites, so DON'T BE PUT OFF BY THE OLD-FASHIONED GOTHIC SCRIPT AND SEEMINGLY DIFFICULT LABELS. The faint-hearted can always turn back to a boring big brand from Australia – be brave and give these hidden treasures a try!

■ Sample a fine German white wine and you will NEVER BUY THE CHEAP AND NASTY BOTTLES from the same country again. German wine is divided into the great and the gruesome – AVOID THE BLAND COMMERCIAL CHEAPIES.

■ VENTURE FURTHER AFIELD AND TRY LIGHT, DRY WHITES FROM UNUSUAL PLACES like Hungary, Austria, northern Italy and Switzerland, not just those from France and Germany.

■ Never try to pair the light, dry whites with very rich food – they will be overpowered by roast turkey and all the trimmings, or spicy sausages and gravy – so STICK TO LIGHT PARTNERS, OR SERVE THEM ALONE AS APERITIFS – these wines work just fine on their own.

IF YOU DON'T LIKE YOUR WHITES TOO PALLID
AND WISHY-WASHY, BUT YOU HATE OAKY,
POWERFUL WHITES, THEN LINGER OVER THE
NEXT FEW PAGES. It can sometimes seem hard
to locate those 'in-between' whites, as we all
appear to be drowning in a sea of rich
Chardonnay or weedy Liebfraumilch. Here,
then, are the medium-bodied whites, many with
ripe fruit and a heady perfume, but very few
of them oaky. The wines that feature on these
pages are either overtly fruity, packed with juicy,
succulent flavour, like New Zealand Sauvignon
Blanc, or they have a spicy hint, like Alsace
Gewurztraminer. These wines have zoomed back
into vogue of late, often replacing Chardonnay
as a more refreshing type of white wine that
still packs a punch. And as we shall see, they are
also amazingly food-friendly, matching the most
trendy dishes around.

You won't be impressed by everything that falls into this category. All styles of wine bring the odd let-down, and in the case of these, it usually comes in the form of a disappointingly dilute bottle which fails to deliver a loud blast of character. Or it can be because the wine is too flabby; it lacks firm acidity to give a fresh streak to all that fruit and spice. Then there is the level of sweetness – often a tricky problem with white wine. A bone-dry glass is expected but instead you get something faintly sugary – or vice versa. The good news is that most modern producers make crisp, dry wines and in the case of Alsace, you can easily avoid the very sweet wines. Then again, the medium wines can be so wonderful that you may not even mind that honeyed tinge.

APPEARANCE

Straw-coloured, heading towards gold
hints, sometimes a little green. Not as
pale as the light whites, but less richly
coloured than heavily oaked or many
sweet wines.

TEXTURE

Medium – not
exactly viscous, but
not nearly as thin as the light whites.

FLAVOUR

Lots of interesting nuances similar to those found on the scent, although good fresh fruit should be at the core. Should have a clean, crisp finish.

AROMA

Terrific! Fruity whites have citrus or tropical fruits or apple leaping out of the glass. Grass, green pepper, even tomato leaves can be found, too. Sauvignon Blanc can be very pungent, with ripe gooseberry, asparagus and even a hint of tom-cat or sweat. Spicy whites have a heady, exotic perfume. A scent of roses is often found, along with cake spices (nutmeg, ginger), lychees… even Turkish delight.

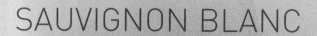

SAUVIGNON BLANC

REFRESHING, RACY, AROMATIC

More and more of us are waking up to the joys of Sauvignon Blanc in all its manifestations. A few years ago Chardonnay seemed to be everywhere and the only famous and popular style of Sauvignon Blanc was Sancerre. Now Sauvignon (you don't need to say 'blanc' all the time) has stepped out from Chardonnay's shadow and become a fashionable grape variety sourced from many countries. It's well-loved partly because it offers a different, racier, leaner mouthful than Chardonnay, and partly because it's rarely barrel-aged, so it appeals to those who dislike oak. But be aware: there's a wide range of Sauvignon out there.

Some of the most famous wines made from this variety, like the Sauvignons from the cool Loire Valley in France, are distinctly subtle and elegant, and as such, they were dealt with in the first section of this book, along with the bracingly fresh and light Sauvignons of Austria and northern Italy (see pages 24-27). Although these wines have a certain clean, lemony quality, they could not be described as fruit-driven and ripe. Anyone who has tried a Sauvignon Blanc from the southern hemisphere however, will know that these are more extrovert wines. Most warm-climate Sauvignons are ultra-fruity, richly aromatic and packed with bright, vivacious perfume and flavour. There are plenty of Sauvignons that hover between the reserved French and the louder New Zealand styles, but generally speaking, most New World examples fall firmly into the fruity category. And these are the wines that have woken up the modern world to Sauvignon Blanc and just what a refreshing thrill it can provide.

NEW ZEALAND

New Zealand's wines weren't famous for anything much until Marlborough Sauvignon Blanc hit the scene. Back in the seventies, this was a winemaking country that turned out some reasonable whites but that didn't wow the critics. The beautiful, cool, Marlborough region in the South Island was mainly covered in fields and sheep, not vines. Then something remarkable happened. A couple of wineries thought it would be a great idea to plant the Sauvignon Blanc grape – best known for making decent dry whites in France's Loire Valley and Bordeaux region – in the stony, well-drained soils of Marlborough's valleys. They reckoned that the low night-time temperatures there and the long, gradual ripening season, as well as that rocky terrain, might just produce decent white wine from this grape. And they were right.

It's still hard to believe that Marlborough Sauvignon only hit our shop shelves in the eighties. It seems like a style of wine that has always been there – a classic. Although it is still a newcomer (compared to Sancerre, Bordeaux Sauvignon and Pouilly-Fumé) that is exactly what it has become: a modern classic, a new type of white wine made by planting a traditional French grape variety in a totally different part of the world. The Sauvignon from this little corner of a small island in the Antipodes took everyone by storm. From the very first sniff of crunchy, fresh gooseberries to the underlying hints of tomato leaf, herbs, grass, tom-cat (yes, really, but it's not as bad as it sounds), asparagus and passion-fruit, New Zealand Sauvignon is utterly distinctive.

It's possible to get bored with that relentless, rather over-the-top, pungent gooseberry character, but most wine-lovers return to New Zealand Sauvignon sooner or later for a reminder of just how vibrant and bright white wine can be. It's a great antidote to dull, insipid whites (of which far too many examples still exist). Ring the changes to some extent by trying examples from other parts of New Zealand. Although Marlborough still remains the most important region for Sauvignon (many, many wineries now make it there and the sheep have had to find new pastures), other spots on both islands do well with this grape, too. Still on the South Island, the regions of Nelson near Marlborough and Waipara/Canterbury near the town of Christchurch, are important sources of Sauvignon (expect a slightly leaner, crisper character from Canterbury), while on the North Island, Martinborough (or Wairarapa, as it is known) is the source of some very impressive, savoury and rich Sauvignon.

Don't stick to just one winery, either, even if it is a fashionable label. There are plenty of quality wines to choose from, so taste around New Zealand Sauvignon. A few Sauvignons have a small amount of Sémillon in the blend; others are made with a proportion aged in oak for a short time, for a subtle roundness; still more are deliberately turned out lean, herbaceous and grassy. The most famous New Zealand wine of all, the cultish Cloudy Bay Sauvignon Blanc, is still on fine form, though it can be horribly expensive to buy in restaurants. Some of the cheaper New Zealand Sauvignons offer better value for money, for example Villa Maria's Private Bin, Montana's range and Babich.

SOUTH AFRICA

South Africa is going great guns with Sauvignon at the moment. Although the Cape's wine industry fell behind the rest of the world during the dark days of apartheid, there is now a new sense of excitement about South African wine, and Sauvignon is emerging as one of the most successful white grapes of the modern era. The style of modern Cape Sauvignon falls somewhere between the elegance of the Loire wines and the richer fruitiness of New Zealand – perfect for drinkers who find one too restrained and the other too overtly pungent. Tasters may notice an attractive lime and passion-fruit streak and possibly a hint of green capsicum, rather than the gooseberry and "tom-cat" of New Zealand Sauvignon. Exciting wine is now being made in several parts of the Western Cape, including the Robertson and Constantia regions. Good brands to try: Springfield, Klein Constantia and Vergelegen.

CHILE

Unfortunately, it's not always possible to know when you are getting true Sauvignon Blanc from Chile, despite what's on the label. The problem is that many of Chile's Sauvignon vineyards have been found to contain a quite different variety called Sauvignonasse, which tastes similar when first made but tires quickly, growing fruitless and flat in flavour. That said, a reputable winery should be providing one hundred percent Sauvignon Blanc, and some Chilean examples are delicious, bone-dry and zippily fresh, with crisp gooseberry and lime and occasionally a slight savoury edge. The cool Casablanca Valley region makes some of the best. Go for Viña Casablanca or the good-value 35 South and Miguel Torres labels.

AUSTRALIA

This is not a grape variety at which Australia excels. Winemakers there have tended to concentrate on Chardonnay and Sémillon, leaving Sauvignon to their Kiwi neighbours. It is partly because many of Australia's top vineyard sites are simply too hot for Sauvignon, which needs a cooler touch if it is to remain racy and crisp. Still, the Australians are now looking to make more elegant wines alongside their traditional blockbusters, and so Sauvignon has become much more popular among winemakers as they plant in cooler spots. The result is some impressive stuff, especially from Adelaide Hills, Tasmania and the Margaret River region south of Perth (where it is sometimes blended with Semillon). Examples to try: Knappstein Lenswood, Katnook or Cullen's blend with Semillon.

USA

The Californians have developed a unique type of Sauvignon and called it Fumé Blanc. This is oaked Sauvignon – so expect more richness, some creamy depths and sometimes a sweet note that will not be to everyone's taste. West Coast winemakers who first pushed this style had fine, oaked white Bordeaux in mind; unfortunately, too many Fumé Blancs lacked zippy acidity, dryness and the fruity stamp of Sauvignon. The style has been toned down of late – more of that bright, lively Sauvignon character is allowed to shine through, and there are certain Californian winemakers who don't use oak barrels at all for Sauvignon. But do tread carefully here until you establish that you like the Californian style! Washington State is the source of a few fruity, modern Sauvignons, too.

REST OF EUROPE

Bulgaria produces some reasonable Sauvignon Blanc, though overall quality is quite patchy. Hungary tends to be a safer bet. This is a country which makes some super Sauvignon: dry, fresh, flavoursome and cheap, with tangy grapefruit and an often rather savoury, smoky note. It is great for everyday quaffing. The south of France makes some Sauvignon in a richer, riper style than usual – the warm vineyards account for this.

GEWÜRZTRAMINER

SOMETHING QUITE DIFFERENT

It's hard to explain what the much-used term 'spicy white' means, but grab a glass of Gewürztraminer (or "Gewürz", as this grape is often called) and the style immediately becomes clear. It's not hot, peppery chilli spice, of course, but an exotic, gingery appeal, with hints of peach skin, rosewater, dried apricots, sometimes a note of cardamom and often pink Turkish delight. Good Gewürz is headily perfumed, so the extraordinary, unique appeal of the wine assails you long before you get the liquid in your mouth. One sniff of a glass of Gewürz will tell you that here is something quite different.

To be honest, it isn't for everyone, and even for its fans it probably isn't an everyday quaffer – but Gewürz is fascinating stuff, and like all the spicy whites, it's a brilliant match for certain dishes; in this case I'd choose Thai spicy fish with lots of coriander and lemongrass, or even simple Chinese sweet-and-sour chicken.

ALSACE AND THE REST OF EUROPE

The most famous and best Gewurztraminers of all come from Alsace in eastern France – a region that has mastered premium, opulent but unoaked whites. These wines are full of fragrance and spice, richly golden-coloured and full in texture, often with a high thirteen percent alcohol, but they are not oaky, and a well-balanced example (as always with whites) should have crisp acidity to balance out that weight.

Wines from over fifty *grand cru* vineyard sites (named on the label) are supposed to be the best, but this isn't always the case and such bottles can be an expensive disappointment. Avoiding sweetish wines (or finding them, if you like a more honeyed style) can also prove tricky as there's little to help you on the label, but note that the words *vendange tardive* or *sélection des grains nobles* do indicate sweet wine. Poor Alsace

Gewurz does exist, of course, often tasting 'flabby', lacking acidity and smelling like cheap perfume. Avoid this by picking top producers like Hugel, Trimbach or Schlumberger or try a simpler but less expensive wine from a reliable cooperative winery like Turckheim or Ribeauvillé. Despite these pitfalls – and the fact that Alsace Gewurz is often packaged in old-fashioned tall, green bottles with dense Gothic script on them – do give it a go as the wines can be quite brilliant, and among the most unusual and fascinating in the world.

In Germany, Gewürztraminer is considered much less important than Riesling. The wines are simpler, but prettily scented and often delicious. The best have a delightfully crisp finish; the worst taste clumsy and unbalanced. Try a bottle from the Baden or Pfalz areas of the country. If you like Gewürz, trawl the shelves for bottles from Eastern Europe (especially Hungary) and northern Italy – these can be a bargain and snappily fresh, although nothing touches Alsace Gewurz.

REST OF THE WORLD

New Zealand produces some tasty Gewürztraminer, especially from the cooler vineyards of Marlborough. There's a delightful purity of fruit here – a clean citrus zest, tangerine note, perhaps some lychee – and a dry, mineral quality to the best. Australia makes very few Gewurzes of note as its vineyards are usually too hot for this variety, although cool, breezy Tasmania can produce a subtle, elegant wine. Chilean Gewurz, on the other hand, is successful, especially from the cool Casablanca Valley vineyards or the Bío-Bío region in the south. There aren't many around, but snap one up from Undurraga, Cono Sur, or Viña Casablanca if you spot it. This doesn't crop up much in California, but a handful of decent wines come from Washington State.

OTHER FRUITY, SPICY WHITES

PLENTY MORE TO PICK FROM

CHENIN BLANC

Drinkers of fruity, spicy whites usually like Chenin Blanc – when it's good, that is. This a difficult grape variety to fall in love with, partly because one of the two countries that makes a lot of it – South Africa – turns out so much commercial, off-dry wine from Chenin.

It's worth persevering with South African Chenin Blanc (sometimes known locally as Steen), though, as a superior bottle has a lovely juiciness to it, with plenty of lime and guava flavours, a nice rounded weight and a succulent finish. The better examples of South African Chenins are moreish, crowd-pleasing wines, reasonably cheap and great party whites. Happily, the general standard is improving, and even supermarket own-labels are proving to be more reliable. Among the best producers are Mulderbosch (lightly oaked wine), Ken Forrester and Spier.

In France's Loire Valley, Chenin gets serious. This is where the amazingly long-lived Savennières is made entirely from Chenin; rapier-sharp with acidity when young, it achingly slowly evolves into richer stuff with layers of ripe apple and cream over ten or twenty years in the cellar. Vouvray, too, can show Chenin Blanc at its best, with appley fruit again, and a subtle hint of walnut oil (Vouvray can be dry, medium or sweet). Be warned though that basic Loire whites made from this grape can be a real let-down. Humble Anjou Blanc is often over-sulphured and dilute in flavour, with a faint, wet-wool aroma, like a jumper that has been left out in the rain!

To be fair to this grape, it is able to produce some impressive white wines when in the hands of a canny producer (Huët or Nicolas Joly) and it's also a versatile beast, creating good examples of tasty sparkling and luscious sweet wines.

PINOT BLANC

It's hard to find anyone who actively dislikes Pinot Blanc. This grape produces wines which are easy to drink, soft, fairly fruity in an appley sort of way, sometimes with a creamy quality and a note of almond oil or peach kernel. It is as a food wine that Pinot Blanc comes into its own, slipping down effortlessly with a wide range of savoury dishes. If you are dining in a crowd and aren't sure which white wine to choose, opt for Pinot Blanc. In Alsace, where arguably the best Pinot Blanc is made, the wine is served with onion tart. The soft, almost earthy wine combined with highly flavoured vegetable or egg dishes works very well.

ALBARIÑO

Spain is much more famous for its fine red wines (from Rioja, and more recently Ribera and Navarra) than it is for its whites, which at the cheaper end of the market can be decidedly plonk-like. But one serious white is made in the western extremes of the country. The Rías Baixas region of Galicia, on the Atlantic coast, is the source of a lovely dry white. Oozing succulent, ripe orange and lime juice, Albariño has good rich weight, crisp acidity and no oak. Well chilled, it is a star match for white fish dishes.

MORIO-MUSKAT AND IRSAI OLIVER

These are the also-rans among spicy whites – after Gewürztraminer, that is. You won't get the depth of flavour or sheer excitement of an Alsace Gewurz here, but you should get something of that rosewater, lychee and ginger exoticism, and a crisp, fresh finish. Prices are low for both, so these grapes make an acceptable introduction to the spicy white style. Morio-Muskat, which majors on the floral, scented character, is usually from Germany, while Irsai Oliver, which is usually snappy and dry with spicy peach flavour, hails from Slovenia or Hungary.

STORING AND SERVING

THE MAJORITY OF THE FRUITY, SPICY WHITES NEED DRINKING UP SOON AFTER PURCHASE, AS THEIR WONDERFUL AROMAS AND VIBRANT FLAVOURS WON'T LAST MORE THAN A YEAR. This applies especially to the more cheap and simple bottles like basic Irsai Oliver. New Zealand Sauvignon is supposed to be consumed fairly young, but older bottles have proved delicious: full of tinned asparagus and baked greengage character. Cellar a top example, but drink up leaner, lesser wines within a year. Albariño and Pinot Blanc aren't great 'agers', either, so enjoy them while they're fairly young. But serious Alsace Gewurztraminer can be matured successfully for much longer – several years in bottle gives it a lovely mellow richness – although be warned that the blast of spice softens somewhat. This is one wine that can be enjoyed young or old, according to your taste.

MAKING THE DIFFERENCE

THE BEST SAUVIGNON BLANC IS GROWN IN RELATIVELY COOL-CLIMATE VINEYARDS, SO THE GRAPES RETAIN THEIR CRISP ACIDITY AND MOUTH-WATERING FRUIT FLAVOURS, RATHER THAN TURNING FLABBY AND OILY. But cool climates bring another potential problem: lack of ripeness, especially as Sauvignon is a vigorous vine which tends to send a vast green canopy over the grapes, shading them from the sun. One answer to this is canopy management, when the leaves are cut back to expose the grapes to sunlight and air. By using careful canopy management, growers can achieve sufficient ripeness without having to replant in warmer areas. In an area famous for Sauvignon, like Marlborough in New Zealand, the bright daytime sunshine and colder night-time temperatures bring about well-balanced grapes with intense fruit flavours as well as crisp acidity.

MATCHING FRUITY, SPICY WHITES WITH FOOD

THE FRUITY, SPICY WHITES DESCRIBED HERE ARE NEITHER TOO OVERPOWERING ON ONE HAND, NOR WIMPY ON THE OTHER, SO THEY MATCH A WIDE RANGE OF DISHES, INCLUDING SIMPLE CHICKEN AND FISH. Pinot Blanc, for example, goes with lots of dishes, especially quiches, tarts and pizzas. The richer, fruity Sauvignons are great with asparagus, tomato and basil salad, and rich white fish and seafood dishes (fish in creamy sauce, fresh crab). Albariño is a wow with firm white fish, especially the hake often served in western Spain. Spicy whites are the ones to match with more exotic food – Gewürztraminer with mildly spicy, fragrant Thai dishes, or Chinese cuisine. Try a ultra-fruity Sauvignon or Gewürz with rich cheesy bakes or roast vegetables, as they both measure up well to hearty vegetarian fare.

FIRST TASTE

■ Sauvignon from the Loire Valley in France tastes much leaner than rich, ripe New Zealand Sauvignon, and South African styles sit somewhere in between. MAKE SURE YOU KNOW WHERE YOUR SAUVIGNON COMES FROM. Don't expect them all to taste the same because they are from the same grape variety – Sauvignons vary a lot.

■ Often called Fumé Blanc, OAKED U.S. SAUVIGNON HAS AN ALMOST SWEET, VANILLA NOTE AND WILL BE RICHER AND OFTEN LESS CRISP. Fine, if you like that sort of thing, but be aware of it. White Bordeaux is sometimes oaky, too.

■ Not everyone likes Gewürztraminer; PEOPLE TEND EITHER TO LOVE OR LOATHE THE FRUITY, SPICY WHITES. So it's a good idea to pick something else if you are trying to please a crowd.

■ Do try these wines with food, and not just on their own, as THESE ARE THE MOST CONSUMMATELY FOOD-FRIENDLY OF ALL THE WHITE WINES.

BUYER'S GUIDE

■ YOU DON'T HAVE TO SPEND A FORTUNE TO GET A DECENT FRUITY, SPICY WHITE. Trade up from the very cheapest and you'll hit a reasonably low price bracket where plenty of tangy, succulent flavour is delivered, particularly from the Sauvignon Blanc grape.

■ It may cost a little more, but as long as you avoid the cult labels, NEW ZEALAND SAUVIGNON CAN BE GOOD VALUE WITH LOADS OF FLAVOUR, and is a reliable type of wine.

■ Very cheap Gewürztraminer is worth avoiding – this is where the grape starts to smell and taste like floral air freshener! Hungary makes some bargain bottles of Gewurz; however, IT'S DEFINITELY WORTH SPLASHING OUT ON THE BEST GEWURZTRAMINER FROM ALSACE once in a while.

■ CHENIN BLANC FROM SOUTH AFRICA IS A SAFE BET FOR A PARTY WHITE – it is cheap, reliably tasty and fun, if pretty simple stuff. Poor examples from the Loire abound, but try a fine one from a top producer for a treat sometime, and discover Chenin at its best.

MOVING ON

■ IF YOU LOVE NEW ZEALAND SAUVIGNON, TRY OTHER WINES FROM DIFFERENT PARTS OF THIS COUNTRY. Most Sauvignon comes from Marlborough, but sample others from the Martinborough, Central Otago and Canterbury regions, too.

■ TRY BLENDS OF SAUVIGNON WITH SÉMILLON, as seen a great deal in the southwest of France. Most white Bordeaux is a blend of the two, and the pairing of these two grapes can be sensational.

■ Like Gewürztraminer? TRY OTHER FRUITY, SPICY WHITES – they are much more obscure but fascinating nonetheless. Irsai Oliver and Morio-Muskat should be on your shopping list.

■ Rather than finding a wine to complement a dish, MAKE SOME FOOD ESPECIALLY TO SHOW OFF YOUR FRUITY, SPICY WHITES. These wines are fantastically good with Thai and Chinese dishes, so dig out your wok and make a dish to match Gewürz.

FEW PEOPLE SIT ON THE FENCE WHEN IT COMES TO RIPE, FULL-BODIED WHITE WINES. Some love them, revelling in their powerful flavours and rich textures, while others prefer their whites light and refreshing. Then there is the issue of oak-ageing. Some heavyweight white wines never see the inside of a barrel, but many spend a long period maturing (and sometimes fermenting, too) in casks, becoming even more strongly flavoured as a result of the toasted oaky character leaching into the wine. Opinion will always be divided, but winemakers who are careful to balance the fruit, acid and oak elements so that nothing is overwhelming or out of kilter should always win the most fans.

Ten years ago, robust, hefty whites were all the rage. Wine-drinkers had grown tired of dilute, wimpy whites and the bright, fruit-driven styles arriving from warm vineyards in Australia and California were a welcome shock to the senses.

Suddenly here were white wines bursting with generous, plump fruit and dripping with creamy oak. Then the inevitable backlash followed - we had had enough of these extroverts and longed for something more subtle. Nowadays there are rich whites with (generally) better balance, more elegant flavours and crisper acidity to counteract those bold, 'in-yer-face' fruit and oak flavours.

The key to enjoying richer whites is to open them at the right moment. Blockbuster Chardonnays and Viogniers are not meant to be quaffed as crisp, light lunchtime aperitifs. But they stand up well to food, making brilliant partners for luxury dishes such as smoked salmon pâté, lobster or even roast turkey and all the trimmings. By contrast, a thin, weedy white would be totally overpowered by these dishes. Hearty food, luxury feasts and cold weather all make us want fleshier, richer wines. So if any white wines can be described as winter warmers, these are the ones!

TEXTURE

Relatively rich and weighty, more
viscous than the lighter whites,
less so than the sweet whites.

APPEARANCE

Bright yellow, hay-coloured; deeper
in colour than the lighter whites with
golden glints.

FLAVOUR

Full and fruity, fairly viscous and weighty in texture for a dry white. Fruit flavours include ripe oranges, peaches, apricots, pineapples and mangos. Buttery, creamy undertones, occasionally a distinct nuttiness. Lightly oaked wines have subtle roundness and a layer of vanilla; heavily oaked ones carry more toasty, sawdusty character. Some older wines take on a honeyed, bees-wax note while remaining dry. Lingering, full after-taste.

AROMA

Richly perfumed with hints of vanilla, cream, rich fruit (especially pineapples and peaches) perhaps buttered toast and hints of spicy wood from fermenting and/or ageing in oak barrels. Some (e.g. Viognier) have a heavy floral, honeysuckle-and-lilies perfume.

CHARDONNAY

RICH, RIPE AND POWERFUL

For many people, rich, ripe and powerful white wine means only one thing: the Chardonnay grape. Take top-quality Chardonnay grapes and ferment them in new-oak barrels, leaving the wine to age there awhile, and the result can be a supremely sophisticated and complex wine, for many the most exciting white wine in the world. And it packs a flavoursome punch.

Chardonnay does occasionally produce light, bland wine, but not often – that's one reason why winemakers across the globe like growing it so much. That, and the fact that they can mould it any way they like, as Chardonnay is easy to work with (it grows well and likes oak-ageing, for example). With plenty of ripe citrus and tropical fruit, tempting notes of toasted hazelnuts, peach kernels, buttered brioche and cream, top examples are some of the most satisfying and wonderful whites ever made.

FRANCE

To taste the very best, splash out on a fine example from the Burgundy region of France. White Burgundy is almost always made from Chardonnay, although it won't say so on the label – as in many French classic wine regions, the Burgundians don't advertise their grape varieties, instead focussing on the village or individual vineyard where the wine was made. Other white grapes like Aligoté, Pinot Blanc and Pinot Gris are also grown in Burgundy, but these are relative rarities; you can be certain that if you buy mainstream white Burgundy you are getting a bottle of one hundred percent Chardonnay.

Indeed, if you splash out on some of the premium wines that come from Burgundy's prize locations along the Côte d'Or – most come from the the southern Côte de Beaune area between Aloxe-Corton and Santenay – you should see what first-rate Chardonnay can achieve: opulent, remarkably concentrated, yet also beautifully fresh and well-balanced wine, the oaky hints enhancing, not overpowering, that gorgeous, mouth-filling, honeyed-yet-dry fruit. Wines to try – and don't forget these names refer to the location not the producer or grape variety – include those from the villages of Meursault, Chassagne-Montrachet, Puligny-Montrachet, Aloxe-Corton, with first-rate vineyard areas including Corton-Charlemagne, Le Montrachet and Bâtard-Montrachet. The best bottles age well, too, losing any hard edges and mellowing to become wonderfully well-knit, the softer acidity and fruit binding seamlessly with the nutty, creamy oak.

Or that's the idea, anyway. Burgundy is a frustratingly difficult and patchy wine region, with big differences between fine and poor vintages, and plenty of inferior wine as well as those true stars. Even Burgundy connoisseurs acknowledge that quality can be uneven, for whites as well as reds. Since the best wines are so expensive, it's important to pick a top producer and mug up on the good years. For the record, 1997, 1999, and 2000 through to 2004 were all good. Try to spend a bit extra now and again and sample pricier white burgundy, as it only gets great once it gets expensive. This is partly because all the top vineyards (classified as *grands crus*, the great growths – the top spots – followed by the *premiers crus* areas) can only produce a small amount of wine, and international demand for it is, of course, very high. But these are wines well worth saving up for.

Trawl around the cheaper white burgundies and, sadly, you will be in for a few disappointments, especially if you have sampled the great and glorious of the region. Those from the Côte Chalonnais, such as Rully, Montagny and Mercurey, can be reasonably good value, offering fresh, quality white at a less-scary price than the Côte d'Or. But Chardonnays from the vast vineyards of the Mâconnais area can be very unreliable; basic Mâcon Blanc in particular is a dodgy way to part with your money and can taste thin and raw. Do try burgundies labelled Pouilly-Fuissé, though, from a superior part of the Mâcon – they are often satisfyingly creamy and rich, and St-Véran provides some decent, good-value stuff in the mid-price bracket. Even basic, generic Bourgogne Blanc from a top winemaker can be surprisingly good: fresh, fruity, juicy and ripe.

Chablis, a famous white-wine area to the north of the Burgundy region, traditionally makes wine that is lighter in style, partly because it has slightly cooler vineyards. In some parts of Chablis, the soil is rich in chalk and clay, and traditionalists believe the best wines are made from Chardonnay grown on these sites

(the soil is known as Kimmeridgian). Chablis is often described as having a steely quality – it certainly tastes a little leaner, more crisp, even with a more mineral edge, than other white burgundies. It is also more lightly oaked, even sometimes unoaked. As such, it perhaps belongs in our fruity whites section – except that in recent times more rich and rounded, ultra-fruity Chablis has been appearing. Expect warm, tangy hints of apple, orange and even rhubarb. This wine is not a true heavyweight, then, but rather represents the lighter face of Chardonnay, albeit with that characteristically generous fruit. Pick a Chablis from one of the *grands crus* (great growths, see page 22) of the region – Blanchots, Bougros, Les Clos, Grenouilles, Preuses, Valmur, Vaudésir – or from one of the more numerous *premiers crus*, the next step down. Quality in Chablis, by the way, is thankfully more reliable than in other parts of Burgundy.

For simpler joys, with less chance of disappointment but admittedly fewer high points, try Chardonnays from other parts of France. In particular, fans of rich, oaky whites won't want to miss the buttery, generous Chardonnays of the deep south of France. These wines (often labelled Vins de Pays d'Oc, country wines of the Languedoc), really do seem to taste sunny, exuding the warmth of the Southern vineyards, which creates super-ripe Chardonnay grapes. But they are 'identikit' wines, tasting very similar to one another and hardly reflecting *terroir* (the character of an individual site) in the same way decent burgundy does.

Most of these southern belles are aged in oak barrels or by using oak chips. A few are blends, but mostly they are one hundred percent Chardonnay. You know what you are getting here; not only is it much more likely to say Chardonnay on the label, but you can pretty much guarantee succulent pineapple and peachiness, buttery-toasty hints, and a rich, satisfyingly full finish. They are much more reliable than basic white burgundy, but don't expect great complexity or excitement. They taste a lot like Chardonnay from newer wine-making countries – one reason why the south of France has been dubbed the 'New, New World'.

AUSTRALIA

Which brings us to the second most famous Chardonnay-producing country in the world. Down Under, in Australia's warm vineyards, an ultra-rich, wonderfully concentrated, luxuriously ripe form of Chardonnay has proved extremely popular around the world. It used to be almost too much, leaving you with a mouthful of sawdust and vanilla. 'Blockbuster' was the word used to describe the heftiest, chunkiest Australian Chardonnays from hot areas like Hunter Valley in New South Wales, and the Barossa Valley near Adelaide.

These wines wowed us on first taste (they first arrived in significant numbers in the 1980s). If you had only ever sipped bland, weak, light white wines such as poor Muscadet and Liebfraumilch, Australian Chardonnay was a shock to the senses. What a blast of ripe, tropical fruit! What a rich perfume! What a dollop of vanilla and spice from all that fresh, resinous new oak! The problem is, like most extroverts, the loudest wines get a bit tiresome after a while. They are so heavy and gloopy, it's as though you should scoop them up with a spoon, not knock them back at a party. Recently the Aussies have started to make slightly more elegant wines. They age them in oak for a briefer period, or use older, less resinous oak, or they don't use wood at all, making their wines entirely in stainless-steel containers. Sometimes they source their grapes from cooler sites where the flavours don't get so overblown and where the acidity has more bite.

Among the cool-climate areas to look out for (helpfully, the Australians spell these out on a label) are the island of Tasmania, off the south coast of the mainland, the Adelaide Hills and Clare Valley regions in South Australia, and Mornington Peninsula and Yarra Valley in Victoria. Expect wines from these areas to taste more crisp and elegant than wines from warmer spots, although, with the exception of the ultra-fresh Tassie wines, they still retain plenty of broad, ripe Aussie fruit. Top producers include Petaluma, Knappstein Lenswood, Tarrawarra and Grosset. But despite the rise of such relatively cool-climate wines, baking-hot regions such as the Barossa Valley and Hunter Valley are still putting out heftier, chunkier styles, and the Margaret River in Western Australia is coming up with a refined Chardonnay style that lies somewhere in between. Try the Cullen, Leeuwin Estate or Cape Mentelle labels from the latter.

Despite these advances, some very rich Australian Chardonnays are still around, and they are great with food such as the most luxurious lobster, the creamiest fish sauces, smoked salmon or roast turkey. But they're too much on their own as aperitifs. The new lighter styles (still big, but not *so* big) are fresher, more balanced more thirst-quenching, more restrained. The latest trend is towards regional characteristics, Burgundy-style, so watch out for marked differences in wines from the far-flung Aussie wine regions. Try a few to see which suits you best.

Blends of Chardonnay with the Sémillon grape are common in Australia. These are no great shakes, almost seeming like simpler, 'dumb-blonde' versions of the straight Chardonnays. But they are generally clean, bright and have enough of that sunny fruit. Prices are pretty low too. Appealing crowd-pleasers, they usually go down well at a party.

REST OF WORLD

In California, it has been a similar story with Chardonnay. The West Coast winemakers used to make hugely successful, monster Chardonnay that you could almost cut with a knife, but they are now turning to a more subtle style and growing grapes in cooler vineyard areas for more restrained flavours and fresher streaks of acidity. The best examples now rival anything made in France and Australia, although they are mightily expensive.

At the cheaper end, California Chardonnay can taste a bit over-oaky, sweet and bland. Not really to everyone's taste, especially if you are used to drinking more sophisticated fare! In between lie some impressive Chardonnays, fairly full-on in character and also heavily oaked, but better balanced by riper flavours of concentrated pineapple and peach, and a crisp finish. And do splash out on premium West Coast wines once in a while – they are sublime, they age well for years, and are a must for those who love big whites. Try examples from the Carneros region, Russian River or the Sonoma Coast for poised, balanced bottles. Top names include Au Bon Climat, Beringer, Saintsbury, Kistler, and Hess. Avoid big, inexpensive brands.

South Africa is rapidly improving, making newly impressive Chardonnays. The Western Cape's wineries, which fell behind the times during apartheid and an estranged overseas market, have been a long time catching up, but today anyone who is a fan of the upfront and oaky style of white wine should give Cape Chardonnay a go – look for ones from the Robertson, Stellenbosch and Paarl regions for a taste of the best. These wines are typically rich and no-nonsense examples, but with well-controlled, rounded oak structure.

New Zealand is another source of fine Chardonnay. Its warmer areas (Gisborne and Hawke's Bay on the North Island) produce richer wines with a tropical-fruit edge; the cooler spots like Marlborough on the South Island, make a crisper, more citric version, but they are all typically packed with a juicy, pure flavour. Perhaps because of the fame of New Zealand's Sauvignon Blanc, its Chardonnay has often been forgotten in the rush, so don't miss out. Some of the most important wineries (Villa Maria, Te Mata, Sileni, Palliser, Hunter's, Cloudy Bay) make excellent Chardonnays. Try to sample wines from different regions, including Martinborough on the North Island and Central Otago on the South, if you can.

Then there's South America, and Chile, origin of so much good-value Chardonnay. If you want lots of fruit for your money, and a reliable source of fresh, clean white with a nicely judged edge of oak, give Chilean Chardonnay a whirl. There are a few super-premium, more pricey Chilean wines around, too, which prove that the country can make top stuff. And go for the new kid on the Chardonnay block: Argentina, now impressing us with its new, highly modern, bright and big Chardonnays at heart-warmingly low prices.

Don't be fooled into thinking that Europe's sole Chardonnay stronghold is France – even though the shop shelves are groaning with French examples. In fact, if you like plump, rich Chardonnay, you should look into the bastion of good-value bottles that is Eastern Europe. Bulgaria and Hungary both turn out reasonably good, clean and tasty versions; nothing very special, but since they are cheap, they're fine for everyday quaffing. Don't expect anything fantastically rich and powerful, however. Soft, fruity and simple is the name of the game here. In Italy,

however, things get more serious with the richly oaked premium wines made in Tuscany, and the highly modern, Aussie taste-alikes from the hot vineyards of Sicily. Spain and Portugal major in other styles of wine, but there are still a number of well-made, almost-serious, oaked Chardonnays about. One surprising source of high-class, judiciously oaked Chardonnay is Austria. The Austrians sometimes call this grape Morillon, and best examples come from the Wachau and Styria regions. These little-known gems are a rarity on the export market – so if you see one, snap it up! Even rarer outside its country of origin is Canadian Chardonnay but that, too, can be serious stuff with incisive acidity to balance the richness. And if you see one of China's buttery, oaked Chardonnays, give it a whirl; a small handful is now being exported, appearing mainly in Chinese restaurants worldwide – expect more in due course.

SEMILLON
CHARDONNAY

2001

Sometimes blended with Chardonnay to create limey, buttery, rounded white wines, Sémillon deserves its own listing for the weighty, toasty, almost smoky wines made from it in newer wine-making countries. Sémillon is a chameleon-like grape. Sometimes it makes lean, grassy whites that would be out of place in this style section, but when it's ripe, mature and sometimes oak-aged, it certainly falls into the 'rich whites' category. Then it makes just about the best dessert wines in the world as well. A versatile beast, then.

AUSTRALIA AND REST OF THE WORLD

If it's big and loud, 'in-yer-face' Semillon you're after, head to Australia – in particular the Hunter Valley (NSW) and the Clare and Barossa Valleys (South Australia) for sun-baked, so-ripe-they're-almost-sweet wines which are packed with flavours of preserved lemons, honey, angelica and lime. Especially lime.

Admittedly, the wines don't often taste like that at the very beginnning. They have a more grassy, lean character, although that lime juice usually makes them succulent and characterful. But after a few years in bottle, Semillon comes over all toasty and rich, as if spread with lime marmalade and honeycomb, yet strangely still dry. It's seriously attractive wine, Semillon, and if you're bored with oaky Chardonnay but still hanker after a full-on flavour, then make it your next stop. Despite its appeal, this is an underrated style of wine, set to become more popular as the craze for Chardonnay wears off. Not all the great Semillons are exclusively made in Australia, by the way – a few worthwhile ones are now being made in South Africa and Argentina, too.

BORDEAUX

Sémillon from Bordeaux can be extraordinarily good: rounded and weighty, with lemony freshness, and again, that honeyed, almost smokey/nutty appeal once aged. It's often blended with the zestier Sauvignon Blanc and aged in oak barrels to add extra depth and flavour. The top white Bordeaux in this style can be a knock-out, but be prepared to shell out for it. Oh, and you'll need a good cellar as they take a long time in bottle to mellow out and reach their best.

As with Chardonnay in Burgundy, they don't put 'Sémillon' on the label in Bordeaux, but many whites from the area contain this grape. Not all, though, will be rich and flavoursome. In fact, a lot of cheap white Bordeaux is dilute and tart. Go for the glorious châteaux of Graves and Pessac-Léognan if you want to taste the most serious and exciting.

Sémillon also makes more humble, everyday whites in the wider south-west region of France, again, usually blended with Sauvignon Blanc. These easy-drinking, zesty-grassy dry wines are not expensive and should be enjoyed while young. Watch out for patchy quality at the basic, inexpensive end of Bordeaux blanc and try to trade up.

SWEETER WINES

An extra word is needed on dessert wines made from Sémillon as these are very important both in and around Bordeaux and in other parts of the New World wine countries. This grape is especially susceptible to botrytis (a mould that is key to the production of sweet wines), as it has a thin skin which is easily attacked by the noble rot. In Bordeaux it is paired with Sauvignon Blanc once more to create some sublime, and very expensive dessert wines – the most famous come from Sauternes and Barsac. In the New World Semillon is used on its own to make rich, peachy sweet wines, especially in Australia.

BLENDS

NOT ALL RICH, OAKY WHITES ARE MADE FROM ONE HUNDRED PERCENT OF ONE GRAPE. Others are a blend of grapes, such as Semillon-Chardonnay blends from Australia. These popular wines are reliable, clean, soft and fruity – a little one-dimensional perhaps, but great value at parties when everyone should enjoy their fruity appeal. Then there's the blend of Roussanne and Marsanne in the Rhône Valley, and the winning combination of Sémillon and leaner, grassier Sauvignon Blanc in Bordeaux. Wine-lovers seem particularly keen on single varieties at the moment, but do try blends as well. They are not necessarily any better, but neither are they any worse.

VIOGNIER

For fans of perfumed, heady, full-bodied white, wines made from the Viognier grape are a must. And for every fashion-conscious wine-lover, Viognier is currently top of the list.

FRANCE

All grapes from the Rhône Valley in France seem to be enjoying a vogue of late, and that's where this exotic white vine comes from. Viognier (pronounced Vee-on-yeh) is seriously cool in wine-drinking circles right now. Which is a good thing when you get your hands on an impressive bottle, and a big disappointment when you come across a dud.

The problem with Viognier, you see, is that if it is made properly, with low-yielding vines, and thus concentrated grapes, and careful work in the winery, it is sublime:

a long lingering mouthful of squashy ripe peaches, dried apricots, with a gorgeous fragrance of honeysuckle and white blossom. No other wine conjures up heady late summer so well.

But, sadly, there are lots of dilute versions around which don't have much perfume, and which are insipid or taste of artificial pear-drops. These have simply been made from vines with high yields of grapes, which may be fine for the grower who wants to sell a lot of fruit, but means that the resulting wine lacks that all-important perfumed peachiness. Sometimes a flabby and disappointing Viognier means it has become too ripe, losing its crispness and concentration. You get the picture – Viognier needs attention in the vineyard and it is not always great, although when you catch the scent of a good one, you'll see what all the fuss is about.

To make sure you get that natural peachy fruit and lovely aroma, pick one from the Condrieu area of the Rhône. These wines are opulent, intense and heady…and extremely expensive. The south of France, especially the Languedoc, makes cheaper, less concentrated versions. These offer a reasonable introduction to Viognier, but avoid bargain-basement ones which can lack acidity and can be disappointingly dull. Viognier is sometimes blended into red wines to add perfume and elegance, particularly in the Rhône. Look out for it added to Syrah there – and recently to a few Shirazes in the New World.

REST OF THE WORLD
Since Viognier became so sought-after, it hasn't been a surprise to see the newer wine-producing countries have a go at it. Most successful is the U.S., where a few decent rich wines with firm, crisp acidity are being produced in California. You might come across one or two fairly well-made Viogniers from Argentina, Australia and South Africa, too. Seek them out. They will be fruit-driven, packed with peaches and held together with a creamy seam of oak. Expect more Viogniers to appear on the scene since this grape is so much in vogue. And of course, because winemakers love a challenge!

Again, beware those which are either too bland or too nail-varnishy in character. Perhaps this is the white version of Pinot Noir – it can be impressive but it can be a disappointment. But it's worth persevering if you like fruity, characterful whites and it's likely more good examples may appear in due course as winemakers perfect their Viognier technique!

OTHER RICH, OAKY WHITES

ROUSSANNE AND MARSANNE

The unusual flavours of these wines are increasingly appreciated. They will appeal to anyone who likes their wines forward and full, but is tired of those modern, bright, 'fruit-salad' styles of white.

They may not be very famous (yet), but this duo of grapes is responsible for the superior white wines of the Rhône, like St-Péray, St-Joseph, and Crozes-Hermitage. These wines are not fresh and fruity in the way that Viognier is; they are full-bodied and waxy, weighty, with a deep colour and flavours of nut oil, peach kernel, spice and sometimes aniseed. With age they grow honeyed. Intrigued? Then try these white Rhônes. They go particularly well with savoury food. These are not wines to enjoy on their own as they taste too heavy and lacking in crisp fruit, but match them with fish or chicken in creamy sauces and they come into their own. Not much is made from these grapes around the world, but watch this space. Winemakers in Australia and California in particular are intrigued by the unusual flavours of Rhône whites, and are trying to make their own versions. A few (very oaky) Marsannes are making an appearance and it's only a matter of time before more hit the shelves. You might come across a big, aromatic Marsanne from the south of France in the meantime.

PINOT GRIS

This grape is very rarely oaked, but choose the right label and you can have another full-on, rich white wine. Okay, so Pinot Grigio, as the Italians call it, is anything but rich, and this grape is very rarely oaked. But try the version of Pinot Gris made in Alsace, in eastern France, and bingo! You've got another full-on white wine. The grape is often called Tokay-Pinot Gris here, although it has nothing to do with the sweet wine called Tokay made in Hungary. Here we're talking about a rounded, almost fat white wine, that looks thickly textured in the glass, and is mouth-filling and weighty on the palate. It smells and tastes smoky, spicy, orangey, dry yet ripe, and it is great with rich food such as smooth pâté, confit de canard, roast goose. Not a wishy-washy wine at all, and a million miles away in style from other crisp, light Pinot Gris made around the world (for more on these see pages 30-31).

VIURA/MALVASIA

No chapter on rich whites would be complete without mention of one of the most rich, sultry and heavily oaked dry wines of all time: classic white Rioja. Made in the north of Spain mainly from the local Viura grape, with the help of Malvasia and Garnacho Blanco grapes in the blend, this wine won't please everyone. Deep yellow, waxily thick, reeking of wood and sawdust, and tasting of vanilla and cream, traditional white Rioja rests in barrel for years to take on such a big oak influence. It's a classic, old-fashioned style of wine, nowadays winning fewer fans as people expect brighter, younger, fresh fruit flavours. Do give it a try, though, matched with creamy, savoury dishes or smoked fish, which will stand up to the oaky wine nicely. Sadly, this style of Rioja is being replaced to an extent by younger, leaner, crisper styles. Shame – we need all the styles of wine the world can give us if we are not to sink into uniformity.

MAKING THE DIFFERENCE

SOME OAKY WHITE WINES ARE FERMENTED IN SMALL BARRELS (CALLED BARRIQUES IN FRANCE), AND LEFT TO AGE THERE. Others are simply aged in the barrels after fermentation in tanks. French and American oak are the most commonly used for reds and whites – American oak gives a more overt vanilla flavour than French. A cheaper method of getting some oak flavour into wine is to soak oak chips in a vat of wine. This is perfectly legal (although it gives a cruder flavour than barrels), but the use of laboratory-concocted oak essence is generally not allowed.

STORING AND SERVING

SERVE ALL DRY WHITES, INCLUDING THESE BLOCKBUSTERS, WELL-CHILLED, STRAIGHT FROM THE FRIDGE, AND KEEP THEM COLD WITH AN ICE BUCKET. Splash them into large-bowled glasses – perhaps red wine glasses – filling them only halfway up so you can swirl the liquid easily and savour its heady aroma. All powerful whites should be pleasant to drink on release, and don't necessarily need cellaring. Simple wines like basic Chardonnays, cheap Viogniers and blends of Semillon/Chardonnay need opening quickly after purchase. But the top Chardonnays will mellow out and grow more attractive, soft and integrated with a couple of years' age, and fine burgundies grow wonderfully rounded, inviting and nutty with maturity. Don't miss older Australian Semillon, too – it's quite different from the younger stuff: honeyed, toasty and rich. Store all bottles in a cool, dark place on their sides.

MATCHING RICH, OAKY WHITES WITH FOOD

RICH, DRY WHITES DEMAND FOOD. They are not the best wines to choose as aperitifs because they are too powerful. Instead, pair them with roast poultry, chicken in creamy sauces, and full-flavoured fish and seafood such as salmon, crab and lobster. Oaky Chardonnays are great with smoked salmon as the wood flavours chime in with the smokiness. Peachy Viognier is an impressive partner for creamy, mild curries. If you want to pair white wine with meat (pork, beef in creamy sauces), go for the powerful wines described in this chapter, not light, dry whites.

FIRST TASTE

■ DON'T EXPECT SIMPLE REFRESHMENT HERE. The rich, oaky whites should be packed with flavour, probably laced with toasty oak, and with a lingering finish. Not for the faint-hearted!

■ Don't sip a heavily oaked, powerful white wine on a hot summer's day; it isn't a mere thirst-quencher and will taste too heavy. SAVE RICH, OAKY WHITES FOR MATCHING WITH RICH, SAVOURY DISHES.

■ THE BEST POWERFUL WHITES ARE THOSE WITH FINE BALANCE. They have a fresh, crisp acidity running through them, which lifts all that ripeness and rich oak.

■ You don't have to tolerate oakiness to get a rich white as PLENTY OF THESE WINES ARE MADE WITHOUT OAK-AGEING. Try a Viognier or a mature Semillon that hasn't been oaked, or an unoaked Aussie Chardonnay.

■ But fans of the ultra-oaky styles should TRY TRADITIONAL WHITE RIOJA.

■ If you prefer something crisper overall but enjoy the rich fruitiness of grapes like Chardonnay, PICK A CHARDONNAY FROM A COOLER CLIMATE.

BUYER'S GUIDE

■ THE BEST-VALUE RICH WHITES ARE SOUTHERN FRENCH CHARDONNAYS AND THOSE FROM CHILE. Hungarian ones can be a bargain, and South Africa offers more serious stuff at a decent price. Don't buy the cheapest white burgundy as it is patchy in quality, and tread carefully among the lower-priced Californians.

■ Top burgundies, Viogniers from the Rhône, and the best labels from Australia and California are as good as it gets in this style category. DO TRY TO SPLASH OUT on them now and again to see what the very best can be like.

■ DON'T GIVE IN TO FASHION. If you love the older styles of very oaky Aussie Chardonnay, then fine. Or if you dislike ultra-trendy Viognier, don't drink it! The rich, oaky whites have always swung in and out of fashion more than other types of wine as they are such distinctive styles. Stick to what you like – regardless of trends!

■ KNOW YOUR OAK, whether it's to avoid it or to search out oaky whites. Look for words such as barrel-fermented or *barrique/chêne* (France) or *crianza* (Spain) on a label to indicate ageing in oak casks. Some lighter Chardonnays might state that they are unoaked or lightly oaked, which all helps you choose a style you like.

MOVING ON

■ DON'T JUST STICK TO CHARDONNAY. Not all the best rich whites are made from this one famous grape variety. Try some of the other grapes recommended in this section; that way you won't get bored with just one set of flavours. What about Sémillon, Viognier or Marsanne?

■ And if you do buy a lot of Chardonnay, be sure to try out lots of different bottles. NOT ALL CHARDONNAY TASTES THE SAME, by any means. Go for a new region, a new producer, an older wine or one with a less oaky character. Don't get stuck in a rut! Other Chardonnay styles are discussed in the section on 'Sparkling Wines' (see pages 106–141).

■ TRY BLENDS OF GRAPES, TOO – Chardonnay with Sémillon, or Roussanne with Marsanne. Don't just stick to single-varietal wines.

■ The rich, oaky whites can get tiresome – too loud and overpowering. MAKE SURE YOU BUY RELATIVELY FRESH AND WELL-BALANCED WINES, match them with the correct food, and regularly ring the changes with other types of wine. Investigate them thoroughly, and if you are getting bored, treat yourself to a top burgundy or southern-hemisphere Chardonnay, or a Condrieu, to remind yourself how fabulous rich, oaky whites can be!

SPARKLING WINE PUTS MORE CONSUMERS IN A DITHER THAN ANY OTHER STYLE. What is Champagne, exactly? Will a cheap fizz do just as well? Do I always have to spend a fortune on a famous label? How do I open the bottle, let alone store and serve it? Does it go with food? Wine with bubbles costs a lot more than wine without (I'll explain why later on), so it is understandable that we want to know exactly how best to spend our precious pennies.

The pressure to get it right is only exacerbated by the fact that fizz is usually brought out on special occasions. Ironically, this means we often fail to notice its shortcomings. People might sweat over which bubbly to serve at their darling daughter's wedding, but on the big day itself, everyone is far too busy chattering, listening to speeches and dancing to notice a painfully thin and acidic wine in their glass – unpleasant traits they may have spotted had they cracked open a bottle one quiet Tuesday night. Still, think hard, and I'm sure you will remember a moment when an expensive fizz has disappointed. There are plenty of hints on the following pages to help you avoid a repeat performance and instead make Champagne and sparkling wines enhance life's joyful moments.

Certainly, there is nothing else in the wine world to touch Champagne for glamour and kudos. The packaging is often ornate and classy, the brands glittering and famous, the price tag scarily high. It all adds to the impression that you are buying a touch of luxury. But I wish we took sparkling wine less seriously in the UK. Go to Australia and they crack open a bottle of inexpensive, locally produced bubbly on an everyday basis, yet still drink Champagne on a momentous occasion. Fizzy wine comes in so many different styles and at so many different price points that we deserve to ring the changes more often. Let your life sparkle a little more!

TEXTURE

Champagne can be pretty rich and complex, but the high acidity and fine streams of tiny bubbles give a light impression and provide a refreshing lift to the wine.

APPEARANCE

Most sparklers are pale and straw-coloured, although pink fizz ranges from a delicate onion-skin hue to a rich, sunset crimson. The look of the bubbles is important, too: they should be tiny, rather than large and coarse, and there should be plenty of them.

AROMA

There's a fresh, fruity perfume, often lemons, sometimes more orangey or appley, perhaps with hints of peaches and raspberries (especially in rosé). A lot of fizz has a distinct yeastiness, too, which sometimes comes across as fresh bread, brioche or even Marmite! Look out for creamy, yoghurty aromas, as well as biscuit in some sparklers and milk chocolate in others.

FLAVOUR

Crisp, tangy acidity is a must in a good sparkler to give a refreshing, mouth-watering finish. As with the aromas, that fresh, clean fruit should be there, and the same hints of yeast, yoghurt and chocolate, particularly on the finish. Champagne is sometimes described as having a 'double' taste: a clean, incisively crisp attack followed by richer, creamier depths after swallowing.

CHAMPAGNE

THE MOST GORGEOUS
SPARKLER IN THE WORLD

First things first. Champagne is only really Champagne when it comes from the Champagne region of northeast France. Any other bubbly is sparkling wine and so must not use the 'Ch…' word on its label.

At the top end of the quality ladder, the best Champagne is still the most gorgeous sparkler in the world. Why is it so special? Firstly, the Champenois have been making sparkling wine for centuries – ever since monks there discovered how to create bubbles, probably by mistake in the seventeenth century – so they have a high level of expertise. Rules and regulations exist to ensure a certain level of quality (though there have been good and bad times for general quality). Most important are the natural conditions in this part of France – the chalky soils and the cool climate – that help to create a thin, acidic base wine. When put through a second fermentation with the resulting bubbles trapped in the liquid, and aged in the bottle, this creates a sparkling wine of finesse and complexity.

The best Champagnes combine a certain amount of power – plenty of rich fruit, layers of rich cream, yeast, bread and chocolate – with remarkable elegance: a fine and enchanting balance. They are among the most effective appetite-whetters in the world, with mouth-watering crispness and palate-teasing bubbles, and yet they also go well with fish, seafood and even light chicken and vegetarian dishes. Some Champagnes are at their most delightful when they are young and vivacious, while others age well, mellowing gracefully into more honeyed, toffeed wines with a mere prickle of gas on the tongue. No wonder Champagne is still so revered and adored around the world. Most other sparklers just seem unsubtle and a little clumsy by comparison.

That said – and you probably knew this was coming – there are plenty of poor Champagnes that let the side down, though fewer than there used to be. The main problems are a sour acidity, high enough to create an involuntary wince, and what has been described as a 'lean, mean, green' character. In other words, a lack of ripeness and a reliance on very young wine in the blend, rather than extra-aged reserve blending wine. In the late eighties and early nineties, these cheap and nasty Champagnes seemed to proliferate. After protests from critics and consumers, the Champenois successfully raised the general quality.

To avoid the tooth-rotting nasties that still lurk out there, give the very cheapest Champagnes a miss (switch to other types of sparkling wine at reasonable prices), but pick a reliable name and never drink vintage Champagne when it is too young. Although non-vintage – a blend from different years – is meant to be consumed soon after release, vintage should be kept for several years after purchase or it can taste raw and tart.

The meticulous, time-consuming technique for producing Champagne is called the *méthode traditionnelle*, also known as *méthode champenoise*, and is used throughout the region. The basic wine is put into heavy bottles, which must be thick or they would crack under the pressure of the gassy wine, then a little yeast and sugar solution is introduced and the bottle sealed with a metal cap. The wine then re-ferments, trapping the carbon dioxide gas produced in the liquid, and the sediment of dead yeast, also known as the lees, settles. The wine is left to age on its lees, which gives it some yeasty character and richness. The bottles are turned regularly on a rack and twisted at an ever-sharper angle, gradually moving to an upside-down position, with the sediment resting in the neck of the bottle. At the end of this process, the neck is frozen and the bottle opened to release the solid plug of frozen sediment. It is then topped up with a little *dosage*, or sweetened wine, the amount and contents of which help determine the style of the finished wine. Finally the bottle is re-sealed, but this time with the distinctive Champagne cork and wire cage. *Et voilà!*

This careful, slow process has been adopted for fine sparkling wines all over the world. Likewise, the same classic Champagne blend of grapes is sometimes used: Chardonnay, Pinot Noir and Pinot Meunier are the only three grapes allowed in Champagne. The first two are the most important and appear either together in a blend or occasionally as single-varietal wines. A bottle that is labelled *blanc de blancs* Champagne is made from one hundred percent Chardonnay whereas one labelled *blanc de noirs* (literally, white from black) is one

hundred percent Pinot grapes (Noir and Meunier). *Blanc de blancs* tends to be creamier with yellow-fruit flavours, *blanc de noirs* has a red-berry, particularly raspberry, character and is firmer and more aromatic. No one style is necessarily better than another, so go for the wine you like best.

The famous Champagne houses do not necessarily offer the best value for money, considering the prohibitively high prices fetched by many of them. Supermarket own-label Champagnes are very reasonable and have improved enormously over the past decade; in fact, many are now sourced from highly reputable Champagne producers. But sometimes we all prefer to shell out more money for a glamorous label. Among the best of the swanky labels to go for – the ones consistently providing the most delectable wines as well as stylish packaging – are Moët et Chandon,

Veuve Clicquot, Bollinger, Louis Roederer, Ruinart, Krug, Billecart-Salmon, Charles Heidsieck, Lanson, Pol Roger and Taittinger. Less well-known but impressive Champagne houses include Jacquesson, Joseph Perrier, the cooperative Jacquart and Gosset. Also, look out for wines made by the grape-growers themselves as these often offer terrific value for money. Good 'grower' Champagnes include Gimonnet and Goutorbe.

The vast majority of bottles sold are *brut* (dry), but do give other styles of Champagne a whirl. To enjoy them at their best, try each at the right moment. *Demi-sec* (sweeter with honeyed overtones) is lovely served with fruit puddings or cakes – it's certainly better with wedding cake than *brut*. *Sec* is in between the previous two styles, so serve it with somewhat sweet-tasting savoury canapés, perhaps pâté or seafood. Rosé can be a delight, usually made by adding small amounts of red Pinot Noir wine from the Bouzy or Aÿ areas of Champagne to the blend. It is fruitier, tasting overtly of red berries and peaches, and goes well with prawns, salmon and lobster. And, of course, it's the ultimate in romantic drinks.

Serve all Champagnes well-chilled and drink up soon after opening; otherwise they will go flat quickly. There are various methods for keeping Champagne fizzy overnight, but, in my view, nothing quite tastes the same as a freshly opened, fabulously fizzy bottle.

CRÉMANT

For Francophiles who don't want to splash out on Champagne, or if you want cheaper fizz to drink everyday, *crémant* is the next best thing. This category of French fizz, created in the 1980s, aims to provide regulated, good-quality bubbly made in the *méthode traditionnelle*, but from other parts of France.

As with Champagne, there are rules and regulations that apply to *crémant* production and, although different grape varieties are permitted in different areas, in very general terms, the results are pretty impressive considering the relatively low prices charged. Crémant d'Alsace is clean, tangy and fresh, rather leaner and more mineral in style than Champagne. Crémant de Bourgogne tends to be made from Chardonnay and Pinot Noir – the same grapes as Champagne – and is aromatic with fruity, red-berry flavours. Crémant de Loire is lemony, zingy and has a crisp mousse. Crémant de Limoux is refreshing, creamy... And so on. Many people discover a local crémant while on holiday in France, so if you stumble across one at home or abroad, then do give it a go.

REST OF FRANCE

Sadly, there is an ocean of cheap and very nasty fizz made in France. That bargain bottle with a plastic stopper, bought in Calais with some spare change, may well turn out to be sickly sweet and artificial tasting or, even worse, metallic or rubbery in character. Buyer beware! My strong advice to those stocking up for a special occasion is always, but *always*, try one bottle of cheap fizz before committing to a boot-load. And do sample a wine called Clairette de Die Tradition or Clairette de Die Méthode Dioise Ancestrale, if you see it. Produced around the town of Die on the River Drôme, a tributary of the Rhône, these are gently frothy, grapily refreshing, off-dry sparklers made partly with the perfumed Muscat grape. They are great with cakes and fruit.

CAVA

A TREAT FOR SPARKLING-WINE LOVERS

One of the most common misconceptions surrounding fizz is that cava is a type of sparkling wine made around the world. It is, in fact, a purely Spanish wine. Like sherry and Rioja, cava is one of this country's great classics. Cava is fresh, dry and fairly neutral, with appley notes and sometimes a mineral quality. It may not be especially exciting, but as such it is refreshing, reliable and remarkably well-priced.

Cava is produced mainly in the region of Penedés, on the eastern edge of Spain, and is made in the same laborious way as Champagne, which is quite astonishing when you consider the price difference between the two. Cava is not made from the same grapes as Champagne, though. Instead, a trio of local Spanish grapes is used – Macabeo, Parellada and Xarel-lo – although some quality-conscious (and fashion-conscious) producers include Chardonnay in the blend to add a modern, rounded and fruity note. Wines are made and aged in the huge cellars that lie under the town of San Sadurni de Noya.

Vintage cava from one fine year is a treat for sparkling-wine lovers. The best examples, from a top producer like Juvé y Camps, taste richer and more rounded but with that same sprightly apple character at the core, and not a bit like Champagne. The enormous popularity of cava is still growing, despite the threat from non-European bubblies. Cava now accounts for nearly fifty percent of the sparkling-wine market in the UK. That's an awful lot of bubbles. As long as prices stay low, and the cheapest supermarket own-label bottles remain so reliable, we shall continue to adore this wine.

PROSECCO

ITALY'S MOST MOREISH FIZZ

Prosecco is Italy's most moreish fizz, made from the grape variety of the same name around the hills of Treviso in Veneto, to the northeast. The best wines are labelled 'Superiore di Cartizze'. Look for the word frizzante on the label as this means a style with a gentler mousse – more froth than fizz.

ASTI

Asti is perhaps a more famous Italian sparkling wine. Snobs are often patronising about this sweet, grapey wine – not officially called Spumante anymore, but now simply Asti – but its many fans find it sadly underrated. Certainly, a fresh, youthful Asti served frostily cold with desserts, cakes, sweet biscuits or on its own at the end of a rich feast is wonderfully uplifting and palate-cleansing. Its naturally low alcohol is a bonus, too, after lots of other, more heady wines. All too often, however, it is served at room temperature as an aperitif when a dry fizz would be so much more appealing. Save Asti's reputation, and drink it at the right moment.

If you still think it sounds naff, try its superior cousin Moscato d'Asti, which is a little less sweet with a softer, spritzier mousse. It is slightly higher in alcohol and costs a little more, but is generally more delicious and is taken a bit more seriously by wine buffs. Look out for the words *Valdobbiadene* or *Conegliano* on the label as these small areas produce the highest quality Proseccos.

OTHER SPARKLERS

PLENTY MORE TO PICK FROM

GERMANY AND AUSTRIA

Germany and Austria both make sparkling wines labelled Sekt, usually from Riesling, Pinot Blanc and Welschriesling varieties. Watch out for cheap and nasty German examples that are often sulphurous; think burnt rubber or struck matches – very unpleasant. Occasionally a tasty example comes along, and any visitor to Vienna may well enjoy a glass of cold Sekt in a bar. There's something about Sekt that makes it nicer in situ than at home, and anyway, its fragile nature means it doesn't travel well. The best you can expect, however, is a zesty, dry, bubbly mouthful. The Austrian producer Bründlmayer makes the finest Sekt I have come across.

ENGLAND

Recently, England has become the unlikely source of some rather exciting sparkling wines made in the traditional method (see the 'Champagne' section on page 118-121). Or is it so unlikely? England's cool climate, which is not so very different from that of the Champagne region in northern France, and the chalky soils in parts of the south make it ideal for producing a simple, tart, base wine for fizz. English winemakers are rapidly developing their skills for sparklers and the result is a bumper crop of quality bubblies, some of which have won awards in international competitions for their poise and elegance. Let's hear it for Nyetimber, Camel, Ridgeview and Valley Vineyards, among others, championing English sparklers effectively for the first time.

THE NEW WORLD

There are now some super sparklers from newer parts of the winemaking globe: New Zealand, Australia, California and so on. There are three interesting facts to note here. One, the *méthode traditionnelle* is widely employed to create the best examples, as are the two most important grape varieties used in Champagne – Chardonnay and Pinot Noir.

Secondly, Champagne houses are heavily involved in the production of much of the finest overseas fizz. Louis Roederer's Californian offshoot, which makes a wine called Quartet; Deutz Marlborough Cuvée in New Zealand; and Moët et Chandon's Green Point from Australia, are all cases in point. Even Cloudy Bay's classy, rich sparkler, Pelorus, has had some input from Veuve Clicquot. Clearly the Champenois know a good opportunity when they see one and believe there is a healthy market out there for both Champagne and sparkling wine.

Thirdly, southern-hemisphere winemakers have only become successful at fizz since they started sourcing grapes from cool-climate vineyards. Hot spots simply don't make fizz with finesse.

AUSTRALIA

Take Australian bubbly, for example. There are lots of ripe, sunny, big-bubbled Aussie sparklers, made mainly by cheaper modes of production than the Champagne method. For refined, well-balanced sparkling wine from this country you need grapes – Chardonnay and Pinot Noir, naturally – grown in cool areas such as Tasmania, the Yarra Valley in Victoria and the Adelaide Hills in South Australia.

Some of the cheap-and-cheerful bubblies made by the less expensive methods are actually fine for everyday glugging; Yalumba's Angas Brut has always been reliably fun and fruity. Also, don't miss the chance to try Sparkling Shiraz, purple froth with soft, curranty fruit. Served cold with a barbecue or even on Christmas Day, it can be a jolly and unusual way to drink bubbly. Okay, we know it's not white…

NEW ZEALAND

New Zealand is an exciting place for fizz. The Marlborough region on the South Island has the right conditions – a long, cool ripening season – suitable for Chardonnay and Pinot base wine. It provides some good-value labels with pure, bright fruit flavours and crisp acidity – in fact, typical of the region's still wines.

SOUTH AFRICA

South Africa makes sparklers by the traditional Champagne method, which it calls *Méthode Cap Classique*, or MCC. Despite the fact that some of the packaging is old-fashioned and garish, Cape sparklers can be surprisingly good, even from warmer spots. Graham Beck leads the way with his range from the hot spot of Robertson, and winemakers from the pretty valley of Franschhoek have come up with impressively fresh and snappy wines in the past. Some inexpensive, non-MCC Cape fizz has been successful in export markets.

These are made mainly by cheaper methods of production and from grapes other than Chardonnay and Pinot Noir. Brands such as Kumala and Arniston Bay may be popular, but lack finesse and character. Stick to MCC wines if you can trade up.

US

California is home to some highly successful producers of refined sparkling wine, made by the Champagne method and from the Champagne grapes. The cooler spots, such as Anderson Valley and Carneros, turn out superb grapes for fizz. Some of these wines are very classy indeed.

There aren't many decent sparklers made in South America that I can recommend. You may just pick up a decent fizz from Canada, New York State's Finger Lakes or Oregon, but you are more likely to come across these wines when visiting the area, rather than in your local supermarket.

MAKING THE DIFFERENCE

THE MÉTHODE TRADITIONNELLE, OR CHAMPAGNE METHOD, IS DESCRIBED ON PAGE 118. Other less laborious and cheaper ways to produce fizz include the transfer method, with second fermentation in the bottle, followed by disgorgement into large tanks to remove the sediment, then the addition of sugar solution and rebottling. There is also the tank method, with second fermentation in large pressure tanks to which sugar and yeast have been added, and perhaps even the crudest method of all, pumping carbon dioxide into the liquid to create bubbles. These methods don't produce such good quality fizz and in the case of the last method, they can make fairly unpleasant stuff!

MATCHING SPARKLING WINES WITH FOOD

MOST OF US CAN'T WAIT TO CRACK OPEN A BOTTLE OF FIZZ AND DRINK IT ON ITS OWN AS A TOAST, A CELEBRATION OR A SEDUCTION TOOL! But hold on a second. Although brut, with its crisp acidity and refreshing bubbles, is a great aperitif, it is also a good partner for light canapés, seafood, fish dishes and, in the case of the richest wines, even light chicken recipes. Try sweeter styles of sparkling wine with fresh fruit and light desserts. Dry rosé makes a good partner for seafood, especially prawns.

SERVING SPARKLERS

The age-old problem of how to open sparkling wine seems to defeat many, including Formula One drivers. There is a technique to this, however, and once mastered, you will be amazed how simple it seems. This is why waiters almost always impress when they open a bottle of fizz; it looks as though there is a secret to it, but they are simply following a few guidelines.

Of course, shaking the bottle vigorously and popping it open suddenly is the worst thing to do, especially if it's a Champagne that cost a fortune! Bubbly is under enormous pressure, so if you don't open it slowly and carefully, the cork could explode from the bottle, wasting your fizz, and possibly putting someone's eye out. I'm not joking – opening sparkling wine and Champagne can be dangerous – so make sure the bottle isn't pointing at anyone. It's best to aim up at the point where wall meets ceiling. Hold the bottle at an angle as it is less likely to fizz up and out in a rush. It's also worth knowing that well-chilled fizz is less explosive.

The best way to open your bubbly is to hold the base of the bottle firmly in one hand (use a dry tea-towel to grip it if damp), and with the other hand, undo the foil wrap and the wire cage. As you take the wire cage off, keep a couple of fingers hovering over the cork, prepared to contain an explosion at any point. Then gently, slowly, twist the bottle one way, and the cork the other, aiming to prise it out gradually. The result is a soft, satisfying hiss as the cork is released into your hand, and very little fizz, if any at all, should be lost.

CHAMPAGNE GLASSES

SERVE IN TALL, ELEGANT FLUTES, PREFERABLY WITH PLAIN BOWLS SO THAT YOU CAN SEE THE PRETTY COLOUR OF THE WINE AND THE TINY STREAMS OF BUBBLES RISING THROUGH THE LIQUID. Fill right up (flutes don't suit being half full, and anyway, it's hard to swirl fizz) and pour gently, holding the glass at an angle so the liquid doesn't froth too much and overflow.

The traditional wide, shallow-bowled Champagne glasses (said to have been made in honour of Marie-Antoinette's breasts) look luxurious, but have fallen out of fashion in favour of tall flutes. This is partly because the bubbles in sparkling wine dissipate more quickly in wide bowls as there is simply more surface area for them to pop up to. Flat fizz isn't the idea at all, so many people now prefer flutes, which seem to retain the sparkle more effectively.

Hold the base of the bottle firmly in one hand, and with the other hand, undo the foil wrap and wire cage.

Gently, slowly, twist the bottle one way, and the cork the other, aiming to prise it out gradually.

FIRST TASTE

■ LOOK OUT FOR DIFFERENT LEVELS OF RICHNESS. Some sparklers are distinctly lean and green with unappetisingly high acidity. Better bottles have a riper, creamier quality, more layers of flavour and a lingering finish. Avoid the high-acid monsters!

■ Try sweeter styles of sparkling wine – *demi-sec* or even the slightly less dry *sec*. *Brut* accounts for most of the fizz sold, but THERE ARE SOME OCCASIONS WHEN SWEETER SPARKLERS ARE MORE APPROPRIATE. Fizz comes in unusual styles, too – not just *brut*, white and French! Try an English sparkler, a sweet, frothy Moscato d'Asti, or a red sparkling Shiraz from Australia.

■ If you ever get the chance, SAMPLE MATURE VINTAGE CHAMPAGNE. Most is consumed too young, so tasting one that is ten years or more in age can be a revelation – a quite different experience to endless bottles of youthful fizz. Look for rich, honeyed, toasty nuances.

■ AVOID ULTRA-CHEAP FRENCH FIZZ, as it is often disappointing. For better quality, go for Champagne or French *crémant*. Always, always SERVE SPARKLING WINE AND CHAMPAGNE CHILLED and soon after opening the bottle. Old, warm fizz is plain horrible!

BUYER'S GUIDE

■ Avoid cheap, discounted Champagne from unknown labels. It may well be thin and over-acidic. Instead, GO FOR A NON-EUROPEAN SPARKLING WINE OR CAVA FOR INEXPENSIVE EVERYDAY BUBBLES.

■ SOME SUPERMARKET OWN-LABEL CHAMPAGNES ARE GOOD VALUE FOR MONEY. Try one bottle before committing to a wedding-load, though.

■ CAVA IS ONE OF THE BEST PARTY WINES THERE IS. It is almost always fresh, dry, crisp and neutral. Serve on its own, mixed with orange juice for Buck's Fizz or with crème de cassis for pretend Kir Royales.

■ CRÉMANT IS A GOOD-VALUE ALTERNATIVE TO CHAMPAGNE. Quality varies a bit, but you should find something palatable for a good price.

■ NEW ZEALAND ALSO OFFERS EXCELLENT SPARKLERS, which are fruity and lively in style, probably the best of all in the mid-price bracket.

■ Californian sparkling wine can be fabulous, but it will cost a lot. SPLASH OUT ON A TOP WEST COAST WINE for a special occasion as an alternative to fine Champagne.

MOVING ON

■ Once you are familiar with the distinctive characteristics of Champagne, TRY WINES FROM DIFFERENT HOUSES, not just the well-known ones. Sample some less famous names and the growers and producers who grow their own grapes. Some are mentioned in this chapter.

■ AGE SOME DECENT VINTAGE CHAMPAGNE. Some people like very mature Champagne, others prefer it more youthful and sprightly. If you can afford it, stash away a few bottles and open one each New Year to see when it reaches the optimum stage of development for you.

■ Don't just drink it on its own, TRY MATCHING CHAMPAGNE WITH FOOD. Simple light canapés, fish and chicken are all easy matches. Try caviar, sushi and mildly spicy Asian dishes with fizz, too.

■ TEST OUT THE BEST NAMES FROM AUSTRALIA, CALIFORNIA AND EVEN ENGLAND, places where they are now capable of making serious sparkling wine. Does it match up to Champagne, in your view?

■ POSH NON-VINTAGE CHAMPAGNE WILL LAST UP TO EIGHTEEN MONTHS, as will the finest vintage Cava and superior non-European sparkling wine.

SWEET WINES

No book on white wines is complete without a word on sweet styles. Although the majority of white wines are dry or off-dry, most people enjoy a glass of luscious, sticky pudding wine at the end of a meal. These are often made from the same grape varieties as their favourite dry wines.

There are some divine sweet wines out there, but unfortunately some sickly, cloying ones too. A fine dessert wine not only has plenty of sugar, but fresh acidity to balance it out and give the wine a clean refreshing 'lift'. When you get a good one – a decent Sauternes, or fine Austrian Beerenauslese for example – you can see what the fuss is all about. There's something about the pairing of a wonderful dessert with a small, frosted glass of perfectly chilled sweet wine that is quite sublime. So what are premium dessert wines like?

TEXTURE Should be richer and thicker than dry whites. Expect a honeyed texture, almost viscous. In some very rich, mature examples, the texture can be quite treacley.

APPEARANCE The majority of dessert wines, including those from Bordeaux, the Loire, Germany and Austria, are a deep, bright-gold. A few sticky pudding wines are ruddy-red or mahogany brown.

AROMA Some have floral scents; jasmine is typical of Muscat. The aroma is fruity; apricot and peach, lemon and orange are common. You may notice toffee or nutty notes, too.

FLAVOUR More apricot, plenty of honey, beeswax, barley sugar, preserved lemons and quinces, with a crisp clean finish. That's in the good ones, anyway.

From France: Semillon/Sauvignon blends, such as Sauternes and Barsac, are enticing, but expensive. A cheaper, simpler version is Monbazillac. Sweet Loire wines made from Chenin Blanc and fortified Muscats from the south are more affordable. Alsace produces sweet, late-harvest versions of its spicy whites, mainly from Pinot Gris, Gewurztraminer and Riesling.

Talking of Riesling, sweet German whites can have great finesse and a fresh, clean character. Try Rieslings labelled Beerenauslese and Trocken-beerenauslese or Eiswein (made from frozen grapes) for the best pudding styles. Austria also makes superb dessert wines, especially from the Neusiedlersee region of Burgenland. Again, some of the top bottles are made from Riesling.

Italy produces, among others, the divine Vin Santo – from the syrup of shrivelled grapes that have been left to dry before being squeezed. Spain offers good-value Moscatel de Valencia, and Hungary the majestic, irresistable Tokaji, made from a paste of nobly rotten grape (see below) added to a fermented base wine. It tastes of marmalade and caramel.

Certain New World countries make excellent sweet wines. Sip Australia's fruity, botrytised Semillons, New Zealand's pure-tasting Rieslings and Canada's amazingly concentrated yet clean, crisp Icewine, made from the elixir produced from frozen grapes.

Botrytis (noble) rot is key to many top sweet wines. In certain natural conditions, the mould Botrytis cinerea attacks ripe grapes on the vine in the autumn. Unlike any other mould, botrytis reduces the grape's water content, concentrating the sugar, preserving the acidity and adding unusual characteristics – a waxy, slightly decayed apricot and honey flavour, with hints of fresh mushroom and rotting leaves – only much nicer!

PART TWO

RED WINE.

THE MOST FAMOUS LIGHT RED OF ALL IS BEAUJOLAIS. This is a wine which at best is joyfully summery, scented and fruity, packed with soft, tangy strawberries, but which all too often tastes tart and characterless. Bad Beaujolais is a serious turn-off, especially in these days of reliable, juicy, warm-climate wines. Recently it seems heavyweight wines have swept us off our feet – think Châteauneuf-du-Pape or California Cabernet – with the unfortunate result that some delightfully seductive and subtle reds have become overlooked. Don't make this mistake. There are certain key wine-drinking moments when a light and/or smooth red is the better choice by far, just so long as you select wisely.

For example, do you really want a blockbuster Aussie Shiraz or spicy, full-on Rhône red when you're sitting outside in hot weather, eating delicate summer dishes? I didn't think so. This is decidedly the occasion for a more restrained smoothie like Pinot Noir or a cool-climate Cabernet Franc. If your palate is fatigued from ultra-ripe fruit and heavy tannins, they are exactly what you should turn to. Don't be afraid to chill these wines a little, either; a touch of cold emphasises their fresh, cherry-berry succulence.

Strictly speaking, not all the wines discussed here are 'light'. Pinot Noir gives an impression of being light. But it can also be concentrated in its fruitiness, with beguiling, intense layers of chocolate, nuts and even cream. So 'smooth' is the adjective that applies here, rather than light. Gamay, the Beaujolais grape, often produces trite, weakling wines, like Beaujolais Nouveau, but the finest Beaujolais *crus* ('growths') have an admirable depth of flavour, plushy and lingering, rather than tough and tannic. So think refreshing and mellow in the case of the most tempting wines that follow. Not necessarily featherweight, but with a certain lightness of touch.

APPEARANCE

Less concentrated and densely coloured than the rich, tannic reds. Expect a bright red-garnet colour, not the black-purple intensity of heftier wines. Very young bottles might have a bluish tinge; older ones are more brick-coloured.

TEXTURE

Think soft and juicy, silky and mellow, without the heavy tannins of richer reds. The lightest, leanest wines taste insubstantial, jammy, even thin, while a fine Burgundy should be velvet-smooth, ripe and rounded.

AROMA

A high-summer perfume of fresh red berries is often found, especially strawberries, although sniff for raspberries, red cherries, cranberries and plums, too. Loire reds have a leafy character and perhaps a hint of green capsicum. Beaujolais can have an estery aroma of pear-drops or banana chews; underripe wines sometimes smell of green beans and mown grass.

FLAVOUR

Those red-berry fruits again, fresh and squishily ripe. There are sometimes hints of earth, game and spice in older burgundies, some say even stables and horse manure! Look out for layers of chocolate, coffee and toasted nuts.

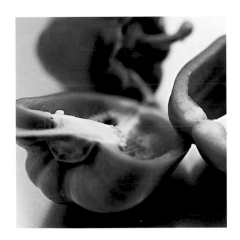

PINOT NOIR

SMOOTH, SILKY AND SOFT AS CRUSHED VELVET

It's not always light by any means, but Pinot Noir is (or should be) wonderfully smooth, silky and soft as crushed velvet. This is one of the greatest red grapes in the world, producing wines with a lovely, lush strawberry perfume and flavour when young, which matures into more farmyardy, gamey depths.

It is also one of the most difficult vines, requiring much tender, loving care and sensitivity in the vineyard and winery unless it is to go horribly wrong and produce an insipid, jammy stew. So for many ambitious winemakers, Pinot Noir is the holy grail – they are determined to master such a pernickety variety and make a show-stopping red from it.

So how do they make great Pinot Noir? This is a thin-skinned grape which succumbs easily to rot and disease, so the right conditions are crucial. It needs the correct soils (limestone is a plus), reasonably dry conditions (dampness is a minus) and the grape-growers must watch their yields very carefully, keeping them low if they want to avoid producing a wine that is too dilute.

Although winemakers across the globe strive hard to get it right, the best wines arguably still come from the Burgundy region in France, where winemakers have had centuries of experience with this notoriously temperamental vine. Plenty of basic (and not so basic)

Burgundy is poor, but the top wines are sublime. Other countries getting the better of this grape are the United States, New Zealand and Chile. If you've had a bad experience with Pinot Noir, don't just give up on it, as when this grape is good, it is really very good indeed, with a complexity, concentration and soft, sexy gorgeousness unrivalled by any of the other smooth, light reds. Just be sure to tread very carefully!

FRANCE

Pinot Noir isn't found in vast numbers across French winemaking regions; instead it is concentrated in two or three. The most important, of course, is Burgundy. Put simply, white Burgundy is about Chardonnay, and red Burgundy is about Pinot Noir. Sure, a little wine is made from other red grapes in Burgundy, but Pinot Noir is what wine-lovers really want from this region: Pinot Noir that is sensual, perfumed and luscious, almost sweet with ripe fruitiness.

Sounds great, doesn't it? But here's a warning: to bag a truly super bottle and avoid the cheap, tart stuff, you need to know a bit about Burgundy and it is not an easy subject to get to grips with. Some Burgundy buffs devote their whole lives to unravelling the wines of this complex corner of France. This is partly because the area is split up into a patchwork of different small vineyards. Conscientious winemakers sweat to extract the individual character of each plot of land, imparting a sense of it in the finished wine. The French refer to this as *terroir* – the site, soil, sun, rainfall, slope – defining the quality and nature of the finished wine. It's the opposite of the large-scale southern-hemisphere, vine-growing region where an ocean of identical liquid flows from the same enormous tract of land. In Burgundy, Pinot Noir is crafted from minute nooks and crannies, and to understand it properly you need to get to know the area, its villages, its most important vineyards, and the characteristics of the individual wines made in them. In fact, to become a real Burgundy aficionado, you should visit the region and drive around, getting a feel of the land.

For those who want to appreciate red Burgundy from the comfort of their armchair, do be aware that the name of the place within the region, and even the specific vineyard site, is considered extremely important here. There are over one hundred appellations, ranging from generics like Bourgogne Rouge to the acclaimed *grands crus* that can be less than one hectare in size. Let's break them down into digestible nuggets of information: there are twenty-four sites designated *grands crus*, or 'best growths', for red wine, all in the Côte de Nuits except one: Corton. Then there are dozens of *premiers crus*, the next step down the ladder for top vineyard sites. All the *grand cru* and *premier cru* vineyards are named on the label. Blends of wines from *premier cru* sites are labelled '*premier cru*' rather than with the name of an individual site, and then there are the wines that come from specific villages such as Givry or Chambolle-Musigny. Finally, at the bottom of the ladder, are the simple Bourgogne Rouge and the even more basic Bourgogne Grand Ordinaire.

Of course, the producers are important, although you would be forgiven for thinking that Burgundy was entirely about parcels of land, not winemakers. Some of the best Burgundian names to sample are Joseph Drouhin, Domaine Leroy, Louis Jadot and Domaine de la Romanée-Conti. Prices are certainly on the high side. It should be said that red Burgundy only becomes reliable if you ignore the bargain basement. In fact, it only becomes interesting and worthwhile once prices are steep. If all the above were not enough to put off the everyday tippler, this is a region of highly variable vintages, so pick wines from a fine year – 2001–04, 1999, 1996, 1995 – rather than a rotten one!

Some Pinot Noir is also grown in the Loire Valley where it is notable for red Sancerre. There is another source of Pinot in France, and that's Alsace, in the eastern extremes of the country. This is a region renowned for white wines, with Pinot Noir its solitary red of any significance. The wines tend to be straightforward, fruity and light, with a wild strawberry perfume and flavour but little complexity. They are at their best served lightly chilled in the summer with fresh salmon: a rare partnership of red wine and fish.

REST OF THE WORLD

Non-European winemakers struggle gamefully with Pinot Noir, usually looking to the magnificent wines of Burgundy as benchmarks and hoping to emulate them, or make a different but equally great version of their own. They don't always get it right by any means; a sweetish, red-berryish, lightish red of no distinction is more often the result, and frankly, that's a disappointment from such a potentially fascinating grape. Still, warmer-climate Pinot is gradually becoming better as grape-growers and winemakers are getting to grips with this quixotic vine.

Sometimes the wines from Oregon impress. The state was heralded as Pinot's 'second home' for a long time in the 1980s, then inconsistent quality and some poor vintages made critics think twice, but Oregon can still come up with the goods. Shame the wines are not cheaper, or more widely available.

California has some success with the grape if it is planted in areas such as Carneros, Russian River and Santa Barbara, where the hot sun is cooled by ocean breezes. Saintsbury, Au Bon Climat and Calera are producers to watch.

New Zealand has recently made a big splash with its Pinot Noir, and certainly some fine examples have come out of the famous Marlborough region in the country's South Island. Indeed, it is good to see Pinot championed by the Kiwis, as other grapes, notably Cabernet, have trouble ripening in cooler climates. Pinot works better, as a recent flood of delicious new wines proves.

Other regions excelling with this grape are Martinborough on the North Island, and Central Otago, a dramatically beautiful area south of Marlborough, where there has been something of a 'gold rush' to plant vines lately. Central Otago's Pinots can be very impressive, with lots of concentration and ripe, smooth texture, but beware crazily high prices for some cult labels.

New Zealand's Pinot tends to be highly fruity, with an aromatic cherry-berry character. Look out for Isabel Estate, Martinborough Vineyards, Rippon and Mount Difficulty labels.

South Africa makes a handful of wines from Pinot that are more elegant and softer than its usual blockbuster reds. Find them from the Walker Bay/Hermanus coastal region. Chile can provide good-value, tasty Pinot, bursting with ripe red berry fruit and perhaps a note of smooth chocolate – recommended tasting. Back in Europe, Romania is a surprising source of decent Pinot Noir, especially from the Dealul Mare region, although these bottles are rarely seen on the shelves. And Germany makes palatable, light Pinot, most successfully in the Pfalz and Baden regions. Here the grape is called Spätburgunder.

GAMAY (BEAUJOLAIS

LIGHT-HEARTED, EASY-GOING TICKLISH

It makes sense to deal with Gamay next, as it is the grape responsible for Beaujolais, and Beaujolais is made just south of Burgundy. For wine buffs, it will never rival Burgundy, but Beaujolais remains a much-loved red, and it can be wonderfully fruity, super-smooth and juicy, with the unmistakeable flavour of fresh red berries. Gamay has been described as the jester to king Pinot Noir: more light-hearted, easy-going, frivolous. Don't take Beaujolais too seriously, is the message, but don't dismiss it, either. It's one of the best reds to drink without food, as its moreish, succulent character means it slips down easily, and it makes a fine match for picnic fare – cold ham, sausage rolls, pâtés and quiches. Beaujolais may have fallen out of fashion since its seventies heyday, but it remains a crowd-pleaser.

That's the best possible picture of Beaujolais, anyway. The worst manifestation is dilute Beaujolais Nouveau, enjoyed more for the ritual of its arrival in the UK in November, soon after vintage, than the actual pleasure of its flavours. Poor Beaujolais (and there is plenty of it) has a smell like nail-varnish remover, a sour-banana flavour and all the concentration of a classroom of ten-year-olds! Happily, there are some effective guidelines for avoiding the worst: side-step basic Beaujolais and Nouveau, and go for bottles labelled Beaujolais-Villages, wine made from grapes grown in better sites, or, best of all, those produced in ten named villages in the north of the region: Côte de Brouilly, Juliénas, Chiroubles, Moulin-à-Vent, Brouilly, St-Amour, Chénas, Fleurie, Morgon and Regnié. These have more depth of flavour, giving a much more satisfying glass of wine, with all the late-summer, squashily ripe, perfumed berry fruit you could possibly want. Georges Duboeuf (the best-known producer), is a good introduction, or try the wide range from Louis Jadot.

CABERNET FRANC

BEHIND THE LOIRE'S BEST REDS

Given the current trend for rich, powerful, ultra-fruity reds, it's not surprising that Cabernet Franc is relatively unknown. This is a shame, as the grape behind the Loire Valley's best reds offers wines with a fresh fragrance, plenty of raspberry character, and even a crunchy, pippy quality as if made from just-picked berries. You can almost smell the dew on the currant bushes here, perhaps catch a whiff of freshly mown grass. The best, though, have a ripe, concentrated core of red fruit (poor wines have an underripe, stalky nature). These are wines that seem to come from mid-, not late, summer, and should be served, perhaps lightly chilled, with a plate of ham salad or peppery cold beef.

Don't look for the grape variety on the label as you won't find it. Instead, find the location – Bourgeuil and Chinon offer the best examples. Try Pierre-Jacques Druet, Joguet, Domaine des Roches Neuves. Cabernet Franc is also grown in Bordeaux, where it's the third grape after Cabernet Sauvignon and Merlot in the claret blend, adding fragrance, in particular. Northern Italy also makes Cabernet Franc, but it's on the light, lean, slightly tart side – one for chilling lightly and quaffing on its own. In newer regions, winemakers have been slow to take up Cabernet Franc, except as a component in a blend, generally regarding it as a poor cousin to Cabernet Sauvignon. But one or two fine examples do exist, showing that fresh raspberry flavour.

OTHER LIGHT, SMOOTH REDS

PLENTY MORE TO PICK FROM

LIGHT MERLOT

Merlot makes a range of styles, most of which are medium-bodied (see pages 182–189). Usually pretty smooth, fruity and soft, Merlot is the perfect blending partner for the more austere, tough Cabernet Sauvignon, in Bordeaux and elsewhere. On its own it ranges from lush, plummy, full, even oaky reds, to refreshingly light, almost grassy, wines. Northern Italy is the source of the most lean and elegant Merlot (or flavourless and insipid, depending on your producer and, to an extent, personal taste). In Bordeaux itself, cheaper reds have become generally a little more fruity and ripe-tasting of late, although some soft, simple, easy-drinking Merlot and Merlot-based bottles are available from the wider southwest area. Choose with care, though; inexpensive French Merlot can still be insipid.

CORVINA

Not a well-known grape, but it is responsible, more than any other, for the popular Valpolicella of northeast Italy. 'Valpol' is a blend of grapes, but Corvina plays the biggest role, providing red-fruit flavour, and sometimes a hint of marzipan. Don't expect great things from basic Valpolicella, but enjoy the better examples, with their lively, youthful cherry fruit and reasonable depth of flavour.

TARRANGO

The Tarrango grape gives Australia its very own take on Beaujolais: an extremely soft and easy-drinking red wine with the flavours of banana, cranberry and strawberry. It comes from an Australian cross between the Touriga and Sultana varieties, developed in the 1960s with the express purpose of providing a lighter red than usual in Australia. It needs plenty of heat and ripens well in Australia's warmer vineyards. Brown Brothers is the producer to look out for. Chill Tarrango well before serving and treat it as a simple but refreshing summer red.

DORNFELDER

Not many people have heard of this grape, but it makes some tempting reds in Germany and even a few wines in England (think aromatic, tangy cherry and strawberry fruit, low tannins, easy to drink). Enjoy these wines when they are young, perhaps a little chilled.

BONARDA

Argentinian softie, making very moreish (at best), very smooth, inexpensive reds that taste of squashy ripe cherries and cassis. Quality is a bit patchy and some wines are on the decidedly light side, but find a good, easy-drinking Bonarda and you have a good-value party red that all your guests should enjoy glugging with or without food. It's occasionally blended with other red grapes. Tesco's own-label Bonardas are a decent introduction.

OTHER ITALIAN REDS

See pages 194–195, Dolcetto and Barbera, and be aware that sometimes these are made in a light, very soft style that could be placed in this category. There are several types of Italian red that count as light – Bardolino, for example, and Teroldego from the north-east. These can be juicy and moreish, at their best, but they are nevertheless fairly one-dimensional wines.

MAKING THE DIFFERENCE

CARBONIC MACERATION IS THE TECHNICAL TERM FOR THE TRADITIONAL METHOD OF MAKING BEAUJOLAIS. Instead of crushing the fruit, winemakers leave the bunches of grapes to ferment whole in vats, until they collapse and give up their juice. This results in a soft, juicy style of wine, as the tannins that are released from crushed skins, stalks and pips do not appear to such a great degree as they do in other red wines.

MATCHING LIGHT, SMOOTH REDS WITH FOOD

LIGHT, SMOOTH REDS ARE A SENSIBLE CHOICE IF YOU WANT TO DRINK RED WINE ON ITS OWN, AS THEY ARE EASY TO ENJOY AND HAVE LESS TANNIN THAN OTHER TYPES OF RED. But these wines go well with food, too, as long as you don't overpower them. Heavy stews, roast lamb and chilli con carne are out; so instead match light reds like Beaujolais, Tarrango and Valpolicella with simple pasta dishes, pizzas and mild cheeses. They have an advantage with creamy sauces, as tannins often clash with cream. That said, fine Pinot Noir goes well with game birds or roast chicken, beef and duck. Choose an older wine with gamier meats. Try red Burgundy with rich, creamy and pungent cheeses, too. Very light Pinot, such as that from Alsace, matches fresh salmon well.

PRODUCT OF ITALY

LAMBERTI

SANTEPIETRE

VALPOLICELLA

STORING AND SERVING

MOST OF THE LIGHTER REDS NEED DRINKING UP WHILE THEY ARE STILL YOUNG, FRESH AND VIBRANT WITH AROMATIC RED-BERRY FRUIT. The richest, smoothest examples may be different, though the most serious Beaujolais (the *crus* described on page 159) will last a few years in bottle and, of course, fine red Burgundy is a great 'ager', turning gamey, pungent, even horsey in bottle as it is cellared, often for decades. Serve these bigger soft reds at room temperature, but the lighter ones very slightly chilled to bring out their succulent character.

FIRST TASTE

■ For those who are unfamiliar with the lighter reds, be prepared for a different 'mouth-feel' from these wines. They are not heavy, thick or tannic. EXPECT A SMOOTH, SOFT TEXTURE AND A FRESH, TANGY FINISH.

■ Before serving, CHILL THESE WINES LIGHTLY to emphasise their succulence.

■ The AROMA IS ESPECIALLY IMPORTANT in these types of wine. It should be a fresh, berryish perfume, appealing and summery.

BUYER'S GUIDE

■ Avoid the cheapest Burgundy as it is likely to be disappointingly thin and jammy. THIS IS ONE AREA WHERE THE PRICIER BOTTLES REALLY CAN BE WORTH IT. Not all are good, by any means, but most of the 'bargains' are downright poor!

■ Likewise, steer clear of basic Beaujolais and especially the gimmicky Beaujolais Nouveau. Better Beaujolais is not terrifically expensive. TRADE UP TO BOTTLES LABELLED BEAUJOLAIS-VILLAGES or, even better, the individual villages, such as Fleurie or Morgon.

■ Cabernet Franc is not especially fashionable, but do TRY THE GREAT LOIRE REDS FOR A REFRESHING YET SATISFYING GLASS OF QUALITY LIGHTER RED. Look for the appellations Chinon, Saumur-Champigny and Bourgeuil on the label.

MOVING ON

■ Dolcetto tends to give a more serious, soft Italian red than Valpolicella. IF YOU LIKE ITALIAN FOOD AND WINE, DO TRY DOLCETTO FROM PIEDMONT together with a rich pasta bake.

■ Reds from Germany and England will only appeal to the most devoted fan. If you fall into this category, GIVE GERMAN AND ENGLISH REDS A WHIRL. Be prepared for some inconsistencies but the occasional fragrant gem.

■ Pinot Noir is the best smooth red variety, and IT PAYS TO SAMPLE PLENTY OF EXAMPLES FROM DIFFERENT AREAS, both within and outside Burgundy, to appreciate how this grape varies according to its site.

THESE ARE THE MOST VERSATILE REDS OF ALL: SOFT AND SMOOTH ENOUGH TO BE THOROUGHLY ENJOYABLE WHEN DRUNK ON THEIR OWN, YET WITH SUFFICIENT DEPTH AND CONCENTRATION TO STAND UP TO A WIDE RANGE OF SAVOURY DISHES. They clash with very little, can be cracked open on lots of occasions, and rarely offend anyone. The medium-bodied reds are much-loved and appreciated for their easy-going character and their consummate food-friendly quality. Have I made them sound a tad simple? If so, then let me set the record straight. They can be wonderful, beautifully made, perfectly balanced and highly sophisticated. It's just that the smooth reds are not difficult in any way; they are not richly tannic, not tartly crisp, and not packed with heavy wood and spice. They are easy to drink, and hurrah for that.

So it's hardly surprising that wines such as French Merlot, Chianti (made from Sangiovese) and Rioja (Tempranillo) have proved so enduringly popular. In fact, it's difficult to think of many who dislike such wines, so I'm perhaps preaching to the converted here! But even if you already know and appreciate the medium-bodied reds, there are plenty of tips that can help you both to enjoy them more and to spend your money wisely. They may be easy-going, but there are nonetheless better moments than others for choosing them, perfect dishes for matching with them, and a few bottles that are well worth avoiding. Read on…

APPEARANCE

Bright and lively, often a vivid ruby-red. Not particularly dense or deep, nor pale and weedy-looking. Some wines are a bit richer and more concentrated in colour, edging towards a plummy, youthful, purple-blue hue.

TEXTURE

Juicy and rounded, with a smooth, succulent finish. These wines should not be too powerful; any heavy oaky or spiky tannins will seem out of balance. Then again, they should have some structure and body filling them out. Look for perfect poise, a balance between ripe fruit and fresh acidity, with some tannin to firm things up.

AROMA

Ripe red fruits galore – plums, strawberries, raspberries, cherries – like a rich summer pudding. Don't expect the dewily fresh, newly squeezed fruit juice of the light reds, however. The perfume of these wines should spell late summer berries, generously fleshy and fulsome. There may be some seductive hints of chocolate, truffles, fresh tobacco, herbs and tea-leaves, with cream and vanilla in oaky examples, more 'green' stalky notes in unripe ones.

FLAVOUR

Strawberries and plums crop up a lot here, as do creamy, soft depths with hints of vanilla (Rioja) and chocolate (some Merlot). Don't expect the spiciness of the full-bodied reds, but there are some savoury hints – soy, earth, pepper – and perhaps a luxurious finish of creamy coffee which leaves you wanting more. Some of these reds, especially the Italian ones, also have quite pronounced, tangy acidity, too: a twist of sour cherry drops on the finish.

MERLOT

BEAUTIFULLY SUPPLE, PLUMP AND LOVABLE

At one point, a few years ago, there was nothing more fashionable than Merlot. Or to be more specific: Pomerol from Bordeaux, which is mainly Merlot; California Merlot; and at a lower price point, Chilean Merlot. Look around a busy smart restaurant and you can be sure there will still be lots of diners plumping for wines made from this grape. They may not know much about it, but they know what's hip and happening, and to some people that still means Merlot. Twenty years ago, it would have been unthinkable. Merlot was considered Cabernet's poor cousin, an inferior blending partner in Bordeaux, and a workhorse grape, turning out less-than-thrilling bottles in other parts of the globe.

So what has happened since? Why has Merlot undergone the sort of image transformation that Travolta was looking for when he met Tarantino? In part, it's due to many drinkers associating moderate red wine drinking with good health. They are keen to glug on red, believing it is beneficial to their hearts (and there is evidence to back this up), but they don't want a tough, hefty wine like our big reds (see 'Full-bodied Reds' on pages 206–243), or a light, pale red with no guts.

Instead, they want plenty of ripe, juicy fruit – a real red, if you like – but one that tastes soft and easy when young, with few harsh tannins. And one that is widely available and grown all over the world. Merlot fits the bill. One television programme on the health benefits of red wine, broadcast in America a few years ago, is widely considered responsible for giving Merlot's popularity a massive boost. Then there's the fact that it tastes pretty darn delicious. Merlot has a thoroughly appealing personality. It may not 'wow' you like a glass of blockbuster Aussie Shiraz, but Merlot is beautifully supple, plump and lovable. It has a friendly, plummy flavour, a smooth, rounded texture. It's too complex to be described as 'simple', like, say, Gamay, but nevertheless it is an easy wine to enjoy. Winemakers adore it, too: it ripens better than Cabernet in cooler spots and although it can make dilute, bland wine if poorly treated and over-cropped, it often obliges with generously fruity reds.

FRANCE

I've probably made Merlot sound too jolly and one-dimensional. Anyone coming to the majestic wines of St-Emilion and Pomerol in Bordeaux, where a high proportion of the blend is Merlot, would beg to disagree. These reds show Merlot at its most serious, concentrated and venerable. In fact, if anyone ever tells you that Merlot counts for little in Bordeaux compared to King Cabernet, then a) tell them it's more widely planted than Cabernet, and b) get them a glass of one of the finest Pomerols and make them drink their words.

Cabernet Sauvignon, Merlot's great blending partner, does indeed hold sway in the Médoc region of France, where its austere cassis and tannin character is fleshed out by the more lush and fruity Merlot component. But on the 'right bank' regions of the Libournais area, and especially its appellations of St-Emilion and Pomerol, Merlot contributes sixty to one hundred per cent of the blend. The rest is usually Cabernet Franc or Cabernet Sauvignon. These wines are softer, smoother, more velvety than Cabernet-heavy Médoc wines, and they are unusually rich, inky and intense in ripe fruit flavour and have an extra sheen of oak from new barrel-ageing to round them off and add complexity. They age well for decades, yet when young are more approachable than other Médoc reds.

The famous châteaux of Pomerol command extremely high prices for their wines. A few are clearly overpriced, the wine often bought by fashion victims. Even so, if you ever get the chance to try fine Pomerol from a good vintage, snatch it! Top estates include Pétrus, l'Eglise-Clinet, Gazin, Lafleur, Le Pin, l'Evangile and Trotanoy. It's trickier to pin down the exact character of St-Emilion as many small-scale winemakers work there, producing a range of styles. Some make such small quantities that they are described as *garagistes*, implying that they make their wine in the garage! Ideally, one would repair to this picturesque town and set to work tasting a number *in situ*. You could go for wine from one of the sixty named *crus classés* (classed growths), but don't expect them to be equally good, or if you're feeling wealthy make straight for the great *châteaux* names, Cheval Blanc, Ausone and Figeac, among others.

Merlot is grown all over southwest France and makes up a high proportion of the blend in cheaper reds. Although it is sometimes (and in the case of cheap claret, almost always) dilute and jammy, it can be reasonable value for money, if you pick carefully. Avoid basic Bordeaux Rouge or cheap claret at all costs. Instead seek out wines from the Côtes de Blaye, Côtes de Castillon, Côtes de Francs and Côtes de Bourg. I can't tell you exactly how much Merlot will be in the blend for each wine, but a youngish bottle that is relatively soft and easy-going, with juicy, red-berry character, is likely to contain a high proportion. The back label will sometimes let you know. If you're on a budget, try the wines of a wider area, such as Marmandais, Buzet, Duras and Bergerac, too, as they are made from Bordeaux varieties, often leaning heavily towards Merlot in the blend. Don't miss the *Vin de Pays d'Oc* Merlot from the deep south of France, either. It may not set the world on fire for depth and complexity, but it is usually modern, fruit-driven, gluggable stuff at decent prices.

REST OF EUROPE

Northern Italy makes a lighter, more refreshing style of Merlot that really belongs in the previous section, 'Light, Smooth Reds' (see pages 8–37). A few quite different and much more serious wines are produced in central Italy, especially Tuscany, where Merlot is one of the grapes used for the much-admired 'Super-Tuscans': a newish breed made with international grapes as well as local ones. Expect quite chunky, oaky Merlot, or delicious blends with Cabernet or with local grape Sangiovese. Prices are high, and results can be a bit erratic, but sometimes the Super-Tuscans do shine, especially those from top wineries Avignonesi, Castello di Brolio, Castello di Fonterutoli and Ornellaia. A few intensely plummy, fairly weighty Merlots are being made in Sicily by progressive wineries; these are reliable, good-value wines in the non-European, fruit-driven style.

Spanish reds are mainly made from Tempranillo, but Cabernet has gradually crept into more and more bottles, and so, to a lesser degree, has Merlot. The Navarra region, a neighbour of Rioja in northwest Spain, has a progressive, modern wine industry, so it is not surprising to see Merlot pop up there. Navarran Merlots are appealingly ripe and well-balanced, and usually a little oaky. Try Castillo de Montjardin or Palacio de la Vega. Find Merlot in Penedés (another go-ahead, fashion-conscious region), Somontano, and even in the blend for one of Spain's most acclaimed reds, Vega Sicilia from the Ribera del Duero region.

In fact, Merlot is stretching its trendy tendrils into almost every winemaking country these days. Austria produces some decent, chunky Bordeaux blends, or mixes of Bordeaux grapes with its own varieties, although these bottles are a rare find abroad. Greece has a few

Merlot plantings, and Eastern Europe turns out some good-value bottles, although these have been rather trumped in recent years by non-European cheapies. Still, some Bulgarian Merlot impresses for its clean, bright fruit and decent oak. It's a shame that Bulgaria's wine industry isn't in better shape, as quality is currently unreliable. If you find a good one, congratulate yourself, as you've probably got a bargain. Domaine Boyar's Blueridge label is a fairly safe bet.

REST OF THE WORLD

Californians have taken Merlot to their hearts – literally, they hope, as they sip the stuff and wait to live that bit longer – and there's plenty around from the West Coast. The worst can be too sweetly ripe, with unsubtle oak and a confected finish, but the best are superb. Concentrated, even chunky wines, packed with plum, cherry and rich chocolate, are made in Napa Valley,

and other areas. Blends of Bordeaux grapes can be serious, too, although someone coined the rather horrible name 'Meritage' to label them. There is some evidence that the Merlot craze is wearing off a bit as punters get fed up with the poor, cheap wines. There will always be Merlot mania to some degree on the West Coast, however – let's hope only the best wines survive any future backlash. Try Duckhorn, Beringer, Newton and Shafer wines. And give Washington State Merlot a whirl, too; it may not be too familiar, but can be bright and lively, as can Long Island's rare take on this grape.

Australia has surprisingly few Merlots, despite its reputation as a red-wine producer extraordinaire. The Aussies have preferred to concentrate on grapes which flourish in their very warm vineyards, hence loads of Cabernet and Shiraz, but less Merlot. More has appeared in the last year or two, and some are impressively fruity. In New Zealand, Merlot is extremely promising, particularly from the relatively warm Hawke's Bay region of the country. As the Kiwis get to grips more firmly with red wines, we can expect greater things from their Merlot. Waiheke Island, a hot spot out in Auckland Harbour, is another place excelling with reds, and Bordeaux-style blends in particular. Successful wineries include Esk Valley, Sileni, Goldwater and Stonyridge. South Africa is another country that is starting to prove it can shine with Merlot – in this case, some remarkably ripe, dark wines, particularly from Stellenbosch, Paarl and Malmesbury regions. Plaisir de Merle, De Toren, Spice Route and Warwick all make admirable Merlots or Merlot blends.

A few promising Merlots are emerging from Argentina, but for now the Argentinian Malbecs and Syrahs are more impressive. Which leaves us with Chile and some of the best-value reds in the world. Chilean Merlot is immediately likeable, its delicious fresh fruit rounded out by a richer chocolate/mocha, even smoky note. Don't expect anything like the sophistication of top Bordeaux. These are wines for everyday drinking – okay, perhaps for Saturday night quaffing! Think medium-bodied, medium price. They are very reliable and justly popular. Oddly, a proportion of Chilean 'Merlot' was recently found to be another grape entirely, Carmenère, which has become muddled up in the vineyards. Carmenère is now being labelled as such, and luckily turns out to make rather good red in its own right, with a slightly more pronounced savoury/earthy character. Try both and see if you can tell them apart. Some of the best Chilean Merlot/Merlot blends are made by Viña Carmen, Casa Lapostolle and Villard wineries.

OTHER MEDIUM-BODIED, SOFT REDS

PLENTY MORE TO PICK FROM

SANGIOVESE

Sangiovese means 'blood of Jove', which doesn't sound especially tempting, somehow. Never mind; it's one of Italy's premium grapes and the mainstay of Tuscan reds, where it forms the base for the world-famous and perennially popular Chianti. There are other grapes that are used in the Chianti blend, but Sangiovese is the principal variety, while Brunello di Montalcino, another Tuscan classic, is made solely from it.

This vine ripens slowly, and that can cause problems, namely stalky green wine from grapes that haven't had enough sun. There used to be plenty of poor Chianti around displaying exactly such a fault, but thankfully the problem is more firmly under control these days. In fact, cast all memories of cheap seventies' raffia flasks from your mind! Today, Chianti, and particularly Chianti Classico, from the heart of the region, is pretty good stuff, aromatic with strawberries, tea-leaves and fresh cigars, and with that tangy twist of slightly sour cherries to give it a fresh lift and make it food-friendly.

The most exciting wines, though, are the riper, beefier, heartier Chiantis – still refreshing and smooth, but without a trace of

weediness. Blends with Merlot (the dynamic new breed of 'Super-Tuscan' reds, see page 50) are interesting and worthwhile, too. For the best of Sangiovese, go for Isole e Olena, Querciabella, Monte Vertine and Frescobaldi. Little is made outside Italy, although the Californians show the most interest and produce one or two excellent examples, such as Seghesio's old-vine example, and straight varietal wines from Flora Springs and Il Podere dell' Olivos.

TEMPRANILLO

Just as Sangiovese is the great grape of Italy's most famous red wine, so Tempranillo is the main variety behind Spain's most lauded wine, Rioja. The Rioja region in northwest Spain has been making distinctive, oak-aged reds for over a century. Don't make the common mistake of thinking that red Rioja is big, heavy and tannic. It is mellow, smooth, aged at the *bodega* (winery) in cask

and then bottled so that it's ready to drink on release. The typical flavours are cream and vanilla (from long ageing in American oak, which gives more of this character than French oak) and hints of aromatic, sweetly ripe strawberry fruit. Garnacha plays an important part in some blends, and smaller amounts of the Spanish grapes Graciano (which provides structure and tannin) and Mazuelo (aka Carignan, for colour and body) are often used as well. In a small number of blends, Cabernet Sauvignon has been successfully brought in, though these wines are officially just 'experiments'.

There are several categories of red Rioja, according to the length of oak-ageing. A few cheaper, less interesting wines will be young (*joven*), unoaked (*sin crianza*) or very lightly oaked (*semi-crianza*), but all serious, traditional Rioja will have seen the inside of an oak barrel for a significant period of time.

Crianza on a label indicates a year in oak, and further bottle-age before release; a *reserva* requires three years' ageing, at least one of which must be in cask and another in bottle; and *gran reserva* means five years' maturation, at least two in bottle and two in cask. Each of these last three groups is worthwhile. *Crianza* is the liveliest of the trio, with more sprightly fresh, red-berry fruit; *reserva* starts to show velvety smoothness and mellow flavours; and *gran reserva* should be a wine of great maturity, depth and roundness.

Variations on the theme include those Cabernet blends, wines with more rich, tannic characteristics, and wines that have been aged in French oak; but to many fans, red Rioja is all about soft, creamy oak and bags of strawberry aroma and flavour. That means American oak, long ageing and the Sangiovese grape. But to make sure you get a bottle you like, it pays to learn the house style of several different *bodegas*, and watch out for those categories of ageing described on the label. The best *bodegas* include El Coto, Marqués de Griñón, La Rioja Alta, López de Heredia, Martínez-Bujanda, Marqués de Riscal, Bodegas Roda, Palacio Marqués de Murrieta and Muga. Great recent vintages: 2001, 1999, 1996, 1995, 1994, and 1991.

NERO D'AVOLA, PRIMITIVO, NEGROAMARO AND MONTEPULCIANO

Here are four more Italian grapes (this country is clearly a maestro when it comes to medium-bodied reds). The first three hail from much further south, where they are the local varieties that lie behind many of Italy's new-wave, inexpensive reds. Puglia is the most important region for decent wines made from the grape Negroamaro – expect soft, moreish, plummy reds, and plain chocolate hints – though you might try the appellation of Salice Salentino, too. Primitivo is thought to be the same grape as Zinfandel, which makes big, gutsy reds in California (see page 234). Montepulciano makes lots of fresh and easy-drinking red in central and southeast Italy. In short, many Italian reds are agreeably easy-going, medium-bodied and food-friendly. Few are truly light or heavily rich. Italian reds make a good choice for matching with food especially as many have a fresh, cherry-sour lift at the end of the flavour which seems to cut through fatty dishes well.

PERIQUITA

Portugal is currently enjoying a new wave of popularity for its cheap, but pleasant reds from the central regions of the country. These are smooth and juicy with cherry, strawberry and red plum flavours although they need drinking up while they are still young. Periquita is the variety behind many of these wines, which are a sensible, low-budget choice for pleasing a crowd at a party. Supermarkets usually stock fair Portuguese reds made from Periquita at low prices.

CINSAULT

I can't pretend to be a big fan of Cinsault, which often makes uninspiring reds in southern France and rather rough ones in South Africa (where it is spelt Cinsaut). But it has its fans, particularly for the occasional new-wave wines that have been made from the grapes of low-yielding old vines.

DOLCETTO AND BARBERA

These are two grapes grown in Piedmont, northern Italy, that live in the shadow of the more famous local grape Nebbiolo, and are not hugely well-known outside Italy. Well worth seeking out, both provide better-than-average, highly food-friendly wine and rarely disappoint. Dolcetto (the 'little sweet one') makes soft wines with a succulent, red-cherry flavour and plenty of acidity – even a slightly sour twist on the end. This helps the wine to cut through fatty food, and Dolcetto is a star turn with rich, meaty pasta sauces or cheesy pasta bakes. It has been described as the Gamay (Beaujolais grape) of northern Italy, although I tend to think it is better than that, and can make some excellent, intensely fruity wines, some of which descend into delicious chocolatey depths. Top labels are Domenico Clerico, Bruno Giacosa, Gaja, Mascarello and Voerzio.

There is less argument today about the sophistication of premium Barbera, plummy and fresh yet ripe and satisfying. Those who find Nebbiolo, the grape behind Barolo and Barbaresco (see page 232), too much like hard work, should go for Barbera. It used to be seen as the source of everyday, straightforward reds, but in the last fifteen years or so some producers (many the same as those named above for Nebbiolo) have taken it more seriously, planting it in better sites, cutting back on the fruit yields, using fine oak barrels to age it. Some of the resulting wines have shown Barbera make the leap to a first-rate red.

MEDIUM MALBEC
Most Malbecs fall into the next category, so see page 96, 'Full-bodied Reds', for more detail here, but Argentina's key red grape does produce some easy-going, mellow, softer wines which are distinctly medium-bodied in style. These offer some lovely ripe cherry and plum flavours and slip down easily as decent party reds or as all-purpose dinner wines that go well with pasta in meat sauces, red meat or vegetarian bakes. Loosely speaking, the cheaper Malbecs tend to be the slightly lighter wines.

MAKING THE DIFFERENCE

ONE FACTOR THAT INFLUENCES THE CHARACTER OF MEDIUM-BODIED REDS IS THE SORT OF OAK-AGEING THEY RECEIVE. Some of the wines described in this chapter are not aged in oak at all, and have a more immediate, simple, fresh-fruit flavour. This may be true of the southern Italian reds, Portuguese Periquita, some lighter Merlots, and Rioja *sin crianza* ('without oak'), for example. Other wines spend time in barrel, picking up nuances of vanilla, cream and hints of spice and cedar along the way. The majority of Bordeaux reds, California Merlots, and Chianti Classicos are barrel-aged. Top Pomerols in particular should have a fine, well-balanced oaky layer of complexity. Rioja is matured for years and it is traditionally kept in vanilla-rich, American-oak casks to pick up its characteristic mellow, creamy flavour and softness.

MATCHING MEDIUM-BODIED SOFT REDS WITH FOOD

EASY! THE MEDIUM-BODIED REDS GO WITH A WIDE RANGE OF SAVOURY DISHES. They don't have heavy tannins, sharp acidity or excess sugar (or they shouldn't have), which means there is little to clash with the food. Just avoid striking the wrong balance. Don't match medium-bodied reds with very light dishes – leafy salads and grilled white fish are out – as they will overpower the food, and don't crack open a bottle to go with a very hearty stew or heavily spiced meat dish, as the wine won't stand up to it. Otherwise, the choice is yours. Game birds, roast poultry, pork and ham, pasta in meaty sauces, roast vegetables, medium hard cheeses, grilled steaks, hamburgers, pizzas, sausages, shepherd's pie are all good bets. Oh, and Rioja is brilliant with grilled lamb chops and garlic!

STORING AND SERVING

THE MEDIUM REDS SHOULD NOT BE KEPT FOR MANY YEARS UNLESS THEY ARE THE STRIKING, CONCENTRATED, EXPENSIVE TOP WINES OF BORDEAUX, CALIFORNIA AND ITALY. These majestic bottles can be cellared for many years and they become more drinkable, softer and more mellow with time. But no-nonsense, everyday softies should be enjoyed within one year of purchase or they will start to lose their vibrant berry fruit flavour. Red Rioja is aged in barrel, then in the bottle at the bodega (winery), and is released ready to drink. Do not age it for years or it might start to taste tired. Serve all the wines described in this chapter at room temperature, in big wine glasses so you can swirl the liquid around and release those lovely fruity aromas.

FIRST TASTE

■ RED FRUITS RULE HERE! Expect masses of strawberry, cherry and red plums. If your medium red lacks fruity character, there's something wrong with it.

■ The body and structure should be well-balanced – neither too light and jammy, nor too heavy and tannic. THESE REDS ARE MEANT TO BE ROUNDED, SILKY AND RELATIVELY EASY TO DRINK when young.

■ Beware the green, stalky medium red. This means the grapes were not ready when they were picked. SMOOTH, JUICY REDS CANNOT BE MADE FROM UNDERRIPE GRAPES. Avoid that label in the future.

■ LOOK OUT FOR CHOCOLATEY NOTES IN MANY OF THESE WINES. They are not just about red fruit, but often about a choccy, creamy, vanilla roundness, too.

■ And MANY HAVE A TANGY FINISH, ENDING ON A MOUTH-WATERING NOTE, or even a slightly tart note. This is especially true of the medium-bodied Italian reds, and, if the tartness is not over-done, it means the wines cut through rich food well.

BUYER'S GUIDE

■ The top Merlot-rich wines from Bordeaux (St-Emilion, Pomerol) and the finest California Merlots and Merlot/Cabernets are extremely expensive. SOME OF THEM ARE MAGNIFICENT, THE APOGEE OF THIS STYLE, but you will rarely find a bargain. These are cult wines.

■ But don't go to the other extreme and buy the very cheapest claret (red Bordeaux). This is often Merlot at its most mundane. SPEND A LITTLE MORE TO SAMPLE DECENT BORDEAUX. Or go for Vin de Pays d'Oc Merlot for a reliable cheapie. Likewise, avoid basic California Merlot, which can be sweetish, over-oaky and unsubtle.

■ CHILEAN MERLOT IS GREAT VALUE FOR MONEY: fruity, easy-drinking, soft and friendly. It's consistent, too, with bags of plummy flavour and chocolate. Don't miss it.

■ South Africa is making some of the most impressive Merlot and Merlot blends for a fair price. SNAP UP SOUTH AFRICAN MERLOT before the Cape starts to charge more for such good wine.

■ GREAT, EVERYDAY, MEDIUM-BODIED GLUGGERS INCLUDE WINES FROM PUGLIA in southern Italy and Periquita in Portugal, with red berries and soft texture.

MOVING ON

TRY MERLOT FROM UNUSUAL SOURCES – Sicily, Austria or New Zealand, for example – to see how its place of origin shapes its character. This is a well-travelled grape that is made all over the winemaking world.

SAMPLE THE RANGE OF STYLES THIS GRAPE MAKES, from light, refreshing northern Italian Merlots, to fruit-driven, warm-climate bottles, to the chunkier, more serious Bordeaux wines.

DOLCETTO AND BARBERA ARE MUST-HAVES FROM ITALY: two grape varieties from Piedmont with wonderful cherry and plum flavours. If you like better-known Chianti, then give these wines a go.

Chianti Classico and Rioja reserva are extremely food-friendly (the first from Tuscany, the second from northern Spain). CHIANTI AND RIOJA ARE BOTH GREAT CHOICES WHEN DINING, and often reasonably priced.

Rioja fans, BE AWARE THAT THERE ARE DIFFERENT TYPES OF RED RIOJA ACCORDING TO THE AMOUNT OF TIME MATURED IN OAK; also some wines are aged in French oak, not traditional American casks, and some are made with the addition of Cabernet. NOT ALL RIOJA TASTES THE SAME!

THE FULL-BODIED REDS ARE NOT FOR THE FAINT-HEARTED. They fill your mouth with rich fruit and tannin, spice and oak, and the flavours and textures seem to linger long after they have been swallowed. Younger wines tend to be chewier and firmer; older ones are gentler and more mellow while retaining concentrated fruit and intensity. Poor ones are either too dilute and jammy or they are unbalanced – too much oak, too much tannin, too much sweetly ripe, 'in-yer-face' cassis flavour. Watch out for wines that impress on first taste, but which you wouldn't drink in any quantity. These are often referred to as 'show wines'; they win awards for their extra clout, but don't always make enjoyable drinking.

That said, if you generally prefer lighter reds, think twice before writing off richer, more full-bodied wines. Like so many styles, but perhaps even more so here, they should be cracked open at exactly the right moment to be appreciated fully, not brought out on every occasion. For example, blockbuster reds do not make great party wines. They are neither soft nor mellow enough to slip down without food; that big-framed tannic structure may only make sense with a forkful of a rare steak. Similarly, they do not suit hot weather, or outdoor wining and dining. Although they might match a barbecued meat fest, their high alcohol and richness can be a quick route to a headache. Stick to medium or light styles of red on a picnic or at a party.

So, bring out the heavyweights to partner robust winter dishes: peppery stews, roast red meats, cheeseboards and rich vegetarian bakes. Used carefully, these make the ultimate comfort wines: soothing and contentment-enducing. Some age well, too, so cellar-owners should take note of what follows. The big reds are like all hefty and daunting things in life: potentially overwhelming but wonderful when handled correctly.

TEXTURE

Tannin – the substance that gives wine a lot of rich body and structure, and an almost 'chewy' mouth feel, like sucking on a wooden pencil – can feature heavily here, especially in younger bottles. Other wines have a more rounded quality, but retain that rich weightiness in the mouth.

APPEARANCE

Dark red, ranging from a port-like, concentrated garnet to brighter, richly purple and even damson-black. Most look intense, dense in colour if you hold a glassful up to the light. Younger wines tend to be a more bluey-purple; older ones are brick-brown.

AROMA

The fruit aromas tend to be blackcurrant and blackberry, sometimes very pungent, like a whiff of crème de cassis. Hints of toffee, spice, black pepper, eucalyptus, tar, treacle, liquorice and mint sometimes feature. Very oaky wines have a strong vanilla character, even sawdust-like on the nose.

FLAVOUR

Fruit flavours include an intense blackcurrant akin to black fruit gums – also briar fruits, brambles, and raspberries in certain wines. Look out, too, for a twist of spice (cloves, cinnamon) and especially black pepper on the finish; chocolate, spicy vanillins and chewy tannins, too. Older wines have a leather or suede character.

CABERNET SAUVIGNON

THE 'KING' OF RED GRAPES

Cabernet is often referred to as the 'king' of red grapes. Why? It's astonishingly popular among consumers and winemakers, it is grown all over the world and, in most places, it makes at least good, and often great, wine. In terms of reliability it reigns supreme – most Cabernet is palatable, and complete duds are relatively rare. It often makes firm and full-bodied reds capable of long ageing, it takes well to maturation in French-oak barrels, picking up aromatic hints of cedar and vanilla, and it blends well with other varieties, particularly Merlot and Shiraz. This is one red grape with which winemakers aspire to make their greatest wines.

The main attributes of top Cabernet are its wonderfully concentrated cassis character, its firm structure and effortless ageing ability. Look out for the former when you sip this wine. A good example will not only ooze blackcurrant but may well have complex undertones of mint, plain chocolate, lead pencil, cedar and fresh cigars. That may sound a bit fanciful, but this is one deep and meaningful grape, and tasters find all sorts of nuances in there. With age (in the wine, not the taster!), they spot leather, game, marmite, earth... Let your inner poet go wild when you describe Cabernet to yourself.

That rich, often tannic structure is derived from the fact that the Cabernet vine forms thick-skinned, small-berried grapes with a high proportion of skin and pips compared to the amount of juice they contain. This produces wine with plenty of rich, purple colour and high levels of tannin. It also explains the reason why certain wines age well, their tannins softening over time. Blending Cabernet with some other fleshier grapes – Merlot, for example – fills out this somewhat tough flavour with more approachable fruitiness.

FRANCE

Red Bordeaux, or claret, may be disappointing at the cheaper end of the market, but few would dispute that top examples remain some of the most serious and exciting red wines in the world. Although Merlot plantings exceed Cabernet in Bordeaux, it can be argued that the latter rules in the region. Red Bordeaux still spells Cabernet for most drinkers – Cabernet filled out by Merlot and Cabernet Franc in the blend, but essentially Cabernet in all its venerable, aromatic, cassis-drenched glory, almost sweetly ripe, dry on the finish, the ripe fruit held up by a firm structure of tannins.

But the world of wine is never straightforward. In truth, a lot of inexpensive clarets rely on Merlot more heavily; the worst tend towards jammy, dilute dross, while in the great Merlot estates of St-Emilion and Pomerol (see pages 184–185), Cabernet plays a very minor role in the blend. But in the Médoc, on the left bank of the Gironde, close to the Atlantic and protected by the forests of Les Landes, Cabernet is the main player in some of the most sought-after and well-loved wines of all – those from the villages of the Haut-Médoc: Margaux, St-Julien, Pauillac and St-Estèphe. Here the vines grow in well-drained, gravel soils near to the Gironde estuary. Some of the glitteringly famous chateaux of Haut-Médoc are Château Margaux (Margaux); Léoville-Barton, Gruaud-Larose (St-Julien), Latour, Lafite, Mouton-Rothschild (Pauillac) and Cos d'Estournel (St-Estèphe). Expect very high prices indeed for these much sought-after wines.

Another part of the region where Cabernet is dominant is the Graves, closer to the city of Bordeaux. The best wines come from the Pessac-Léognan area of Graves, and include the first-growth Haut-Brion. First growth? The Bordeaux classification system is something that all traditional wine buffs make an effort to master, even though it sometimes seems ludicrously old-fashioned and out of touch. It works on a pyramid structure with five tiers of *crus classés* (classed growths). The most important summary of rankings was made in 1855. (See what I mean about outmoded?) Today there is much controversy over which *châteaux* deserve demotion and promotion. For example, some fifth-growth *châteaux*, such as Lynch-Bages and Grand-Puy-Lacoste, make superb wines that belie their relatively low ranking. Make your own mind up by trying as many as possible (though let's hope you are being treated, as prices for top clarets are, of course, sky-high). Those who are impressed by famous classed-growth labels should note that ninety per cent of wine made in the commune of Pauillac is classed growth, and its *châteaux* Latour, Lafite and Mouton-Rothschild are all first growths. It should be said that some of these wines are truly remarkable in terms of complexity, depth of flavour, fine balance and longevity. Then again, some wonder what all the fuss is about. The only answer is to try out fine claret and see what you think.

For those of us who haven't won the lottery, the Médoc region of Bordeaux also produces plenty of generic red wine for a much lower outlay. Here's a useful hint: try wines labelled 'Cru Bourgeois', the category just below classed growth. Within this group, the many *châteaux* are well worth a whirl and often offer some fine drinking at a reasonable price. Or try the 'second wines' of the great *châteaux*, made either from rejected blends of the top houses or from the fruit of young, up-and-coming vines. Taste Les Forts de Latour or Pavillon Rouge from Château Margaux, among others – not exactly cheap, but cheaper.

When buying both these good-value wines and the classed growths, it's important to choose a decent vintage: these not only taste better when young, they age better, too. Recent fine vintages include 2000, 1997 (for earlier drinking), 1995, 1990, 1989 and 1988. For more on the slightly lighter generic clarets and Merlot-heavy blends from the region, see the section on 'Medium-bodied, Soft Reds' (pages 174–205).

Bergerac makes a few wines from the Cabernet grape that are relatively full-bodied, but in general they are softer than in Bordeaux's most famous areas. Some rich Cabernets and Cabernet blends can be found more widely in southwest France, including thick, ripe modern wines from the Languedoc. Generally, these tend to lack the subtlety and ageing potential of the top clarets, with a 'New World' sunny, blackcurrant flavour, but can be good value if you want a modern, fruit-driven wine.

REST OF EUROPE

Spain has proved it can make some impressive Cabernet, mainly in Penedès (thank you, Miguel Torres and Jean León, who pioneered international grapes here), although plenty of other regions are now throwing Cabernet into the blend. In Rioja and Ribera del Duero, progressive winemakers blend it with the main variety Tempranillo for some successful, ripe reds, while Navarra makes some fruity, straightforward, single-varietal Cabs. Ribera's Vega Sicilia makes one of the most famous Spanish reds of all: a long-lived blend of Tempranillo, Cabernet, Merlot and Malbec.

It's a similar story in Italy, where winemakers tend to use Cabernet to make interesting, premium blends with Merlot or the Tuscan grape, Sangiovese. The variety is becoming increasingly important in central Italy, where many serious, concentrated reds are based on Cabernet. This means that the wines fall foul of the local regulations (Cabernet isn't allowed) and therefore can't attain normal DOCG status. These wild-card wines, known as 'Super-Tuscans', are much admired by collectors of fine Italian reds. The most famous are made by the Antinori winery.

Eastern Europe, and particularly Bulgaria, is known for cheap-and-cheerful Cabernet. No longer as popular an everyday glugger as it once was, Bulgarian Cabernet can still be pleasant, with clean cassis fruit, a rounded texture and some creamy oak in most examples. These wines are a bit 'mass-market', however, fairly boring, and not quite as rich as one might hope for. Still, they are doggedly cheap. Domaine Boyar is the name to go for if you want to try a Bulgarian Cabernet.

Finally, perhaps surprisingly, Austria is source of decent Cabernet, usually in the form of blends with Merlot and sometimes local Austrian grapes. The Burgenland region makes the majority of worthwhile examples.

REST OF THE WORLD

In newer wine-producing regions, more premium wines are made from Cabernet than from any other grape. Many winemakers here aspire to a 'flagship' wine that is produced from pure Cabernet or, more usually, a classic Bordeaux blend. This variety travels well, producing fine wine in many sites, as long as there is enough heat for it to ripen sufficiently, as this is a slow developer, and also providing soils don't get too wet. It generally obliges, coming up with that signature cassis in warm southern hemisphere countries, usually a particularly ripe and juicy note, and plenty of colour and body.

Of course, there are exceptions, and those pursuing warm-climate Cabernet should be aware that

blandness can be a problem. Simple, fruity, one-dimensional wines are all very well – if you don't give a hoot for the fact that this grape is capable of so much more. Cabernet is now so overwhelmingly popular that some wineries churn it out as a cheap, commercial wine because putting this grape on a label means it will sell. It's easy to get bored with these wines, and inevitably some wise drinkers will switch to more exciting, if lesser-known, varieties. So watch out – reasonably palatable just isn't good enough from this great grape!

Argentina has been guilty of making Cabernets like this for the past few years and although a few decent examples are made here, there are more exciting Argentinian reds to be had from the Malbec and Syrah grapes (for the latter, see pages 224–229). Neighbouring Chile is much more exciting when it comes to Cabernet. A fine, classic example of Chilean Cabernet strikes a memorably pure,

clear, bright blackcurrant note – like eating a big spoonful of shiny fruit from a baked currant pie. Take into account the low prices of many bottles, and it's easy to see why the Chilean style is immensely popular. Rapel is one region to look out for, and some of the top labels from Chile are made by Errázuriz, Santa Rita and Santa Carolina. It is in the mid-price bracket where this style truly excels; cheapies can sometimes be a bit mundane, and Chile has yet to prove it can make truly great, top-rank Cabernet and Cabernet blends in significant numbers.

Further north, California is the source of some monster Cabernets – monster in the sense of big, brooding, ultra-concentrated wines with loads of extract and decades of life ahead of them. These are wines to take seriously; the top ones can rival Bordeaux in terms of complexity and longevity, although it can be argued that they are a little less subtle, and major in thick, rich fruit and vanilla rather than anything else. Unsurprisingly, they are very expensive and are often snapped up by rich American collectors, who squirrel them away in cellars for years. The best come from the Napa Valley, Sonoma and some sites south of San Francisco Bay; coolish hillside sites producing the most interesting wines. Watch out for some heavily alcoholic and unbalanced numbers, although thankfully these have diminished in recent years and it seems that quality is on the up. Producers to go for include Beringer, Caymus, Hess Collection, Mondavi, Opus One, Joseph Phelps and Screaming Eagle (though strictly for millionnaires). Try Washington State's Cabernet, too – it's beginning to show great promise, with wines tasting intensely fruity.

Australia's best reds are made from Shiraz – a personal view, but there you go. Still, its Cabernet comes a close second. Basic cheap blends of Cabernet and Shiraz can be a bit boring and bland, but more serious examples – you have to spend more – tend to be flavour-packed and chunky. Cabernet on its own varies in character from region to region, which will surprise those who think all Aussie wine tastes the same!

So, Coonawarra is an area well worth exploring, its famous 'terra rossa' iron-rich soils providing exciting, elegant wines which are nonetheless packed with fruit and firm structure. Padthaway, Clare Valley and McLaren Vale give different interpretations; look out for notes of chocolate, eucalyptus, blackberry and wine gums, and make up your own mind about which regional style you prefer. Margaret River, south of Perth in the west, makes particularly compelling, subtle-yet-powerful Cabernet and Cabernet blends. Top producers from across the country include Penfolds, Cullen, Leeuwin

Estate, Chapel Hill and Yalumba. Look out, too, for some excellent, gutsy wines from South Africa. A few years ago, Cape Cabernet and Cabernet blends looked much less promising as many vineyards were diseased. Dull, fruitless, tired wines were all too often the experience. Now, virus-free clones have matured and, in general, South African winemaking has wised up to overseas competition and started to compete more cleverly. The future is looking bright. The warmer Stellenbosch region is clearly the best for Cabernet, with Paarl vineyards a close second. Top labels to try out include Clos Malverne, Vergelegen, De Toren, De Trafford, Grangehurst, Plaisir de Merle and Rustenberg.

That covers the major Cabernet-producing countries, but Cabernet hunters should look out for the occasional gem from New Zealand – with Bordeaux-style blends of Cabernet and Merlot, sometimes with Cabernet Franc and Malbec, from the Hawke's Bay region of the North Island currently the most successful formula. And then there's the Lebanon, where one winery, Château Musar, puts out a blend of Cabernet with the lesser-known Cinsault grape which has become a rich, leathery, spicy cult red. A must if you are exploring this variety – although not to everyone's taste.

SYRAH/SHIRAZ

A WALK ON THE WILD SIDE

Syrah and Shiraz are one and the same grape variety – Syrah is the French name, and Shiraz is the name given to it in Australia, South Africa and other parts of the world. This grape variety is a must if you want to experience the richer, darker side of red wine. Not all Syrahs/Shirazes (or blends that incorporate it) will be satisfyingly full-on, so watch out for some of the weedy, jammy cheapies, but in the main, this is one of the grapes to go for if you want a heavyweight. It doesn't often deliver fresh, fruity flavours, however.

Syrah/Shiraz can be lots of things, but it isn't in the 'fruit salad' school of wine. It's hard to swirl a glass of the stuff and find raspberries, strawberries, plums and cassis, as you will with many red grapes. Instead, potent, wilder aromas assail the nostrils – of spice, black pepper, toffee, cream, herbs, smoke, leather, citrus peel – and the taste is similar. Sure, there is a rich blackberry/

blackcurrant element in certain, especially non-European, Shirazes, but those unusual characteristics still stand out, and are what make this grape so misunderstood and often underrated. It was often used as a 'workhorse', churning out cheap and rough reds, especially in Australia, until the modern era kicked in and winemakers started making first-rate, premium reds from it. Those who liked powerful, robust wines loved Shiraz; a modern classic was born.

Of course, as Syrah, this grape was always much appreciated. The Rhône Valley is renowned for its gutsy, concentrated, sun-baked reds, and Syrah has always played a major part in these. This variety's popularity is set to grow as more winemakers around the world take it on and come up with startlingly good results. Still, for now it remains less well-known than Cabernet, Merlot and Pinot Noir. So, if you haven't discovered Syrah/Shiraz yet, make a point of doing so now. Note it is made in the warmer parts of the winemaking globe, where the hot sun coaxes the grapes into ripeness.

FRANCE

The huge, smouldering reds of the northern Rhône Valley are made almost entirely from Syrah. This is a sunny area that starts at Vienne, with the appellation of Côte-Rôtie ('roasted slope'), and runs southwards to St-Péray, near the town of Valence. The wines are dense, intense, super-concentrated with a twist of black pepper and a rich, rounded texture. Some have a sprinkling of white Viognier grapes in the blend, which gives the liquid a fragant lift. The winemakers of Côte-Rôtie are arguably the greatest in the south, making brooding monsters packed with black fruit and spice, but don't pass up the chance for a decent bottle from the appellations of Crozes-Hermitage, Hermitage, St-Joseph and Cornas,

either. Names such as Chapoutier, Chave, Graillot, Delas, Guigal and Paul Jaboulet are all well worth exploring. The best wines are thoroughly age-worthy, their heavy structure softening and loosening up over time.

The southern section of the Rhône begins below Montélimar and is a hot, arid place where rich, headily alcoholic reds are the norm. The most famous wine of the region is the purple-hued, heavyweight Châteauneuf-du-Pape, which is made from a heady mix of up to thirteen different grape varieties, mainly Grenache (see page 230) but also Syrah and Mourvèdre. Vineyards contain big flat stones which retain the heat of the sun well into the evening. Other southern Rhône reds produced from a similar blend include Gigondas, Vacqueyras and Lirac. Again, the top wines should mature well for years. Further down the prestige ladder come sixteen named Côtes du Rhône-Villages (including Cairanne, Rasteau and Beaumes-de-Venise), then generic Côtes du Rhône-Villages, which are often good value for money, and below that the cheapish Côtes du Rhône reds, which can occasionally please but are often basic and a bit dilute. Château de Beaucastel, Château Rayas and Vieux Télégraphe are all top labels. In the south of France, Syrah is often used in blends or on its own to make modern, flavoursome reds with a black-wine-gum flavour – these will appeal to lovers of non-European Shiraz and Cabernet.

AUSTRALIA

This is the country that relied on Shiraz (as they call it) as a trusty servant for over a century, turning out fortified wine and basic 'dry reds' from it until finally realising it could (and should) be taken far more seriously. Now it is one of Australia's trump cards, producing some of its most awesome wines, much from ancient vines which yield small harvests of wonderfully concentrated grapes. The result is big, powerful, mouth-filling red wine, heavy on the black-fruit pastilles, chewy and lingering, smooth and often velvety in its flavour – the gentle giants of the red-wine world. Australian Shiraz is reliable, too – you will rarely encounter a complete horror, so if you like this style of wine, you are on to a good thing. Blends of Shiraz with Cabernet produce some rather mundane, soft reds, but other compellingly rich bins.

The most famous Aussie Shiraz is Penfolds' Grange. It's an amazingly long-lived, intense red made mainly from fruit grown in the hot Barossa Valley, South Australia, one of the best sources of Shiraz in the country. Grange is not cheap, to put it mildly. In the Hunter Valley, New South Wales, Shiraz has a reputation for being leathery and with an aroma

of 'sweaty saddles', but the vaguely grubby styles of the past have made way for cleaner, fruitier wines. McLaren Vale Shiraz can be honest, big, chocolatey stuff, Victoria makes peppery, perfumed variants, and Western Australia makes cassis-laden wines with subtle nuances of eucalyptus and mint. Look out for these and other regional characteristics. Which names should you watch for? Top labels include Penfolds, Hardy's top wines, Peter Lehmann, Henschke, Jasper Hill, Charles Melton, Mount Langi Ghiran, Tatachilla, Yalumba and Jim Barry, but cheaper own-label brands can be tasty, too.

REST OF THE WORLD

This is currently a fashionable variety, and winemakers are embracing it in many countries, so watch this space as more fine examples appear on the shelves. In California, producers who love Rhône varieties have been dubbed the 'Rhône Rangers' – sample the efforts of Bonny Doon, or Cline Cellars to judge how well they are doing. South Africa is one to watch; some of the Syrah/Shiraz coming out of the Cape at the moment is marvellously concentrated and Rhône-like, with a strong, oaky structure. Try wines from the Groot Constantia and Boekenhoutskloof wineries if you get the chance. New Zealand is a surprising source of fine Syrah – surprising because this grape needs lots of warmth and it doesn't get too hot there. But the sunny Hawke's Bay region is proving it can be successful with this variety. More plantings are set to come on stream in the next few years, so look out for Kiwi Syrah. Another tip is Argentina where wines from the Mendoza region, close to the Andes, are causing a stir for their ripe, smooth character.

OTHER FULL-BODIED REDS

PLENTY MORE TO PICK FROM

GRENACHE

The Grenache grape doesn't excel at making subtle, complex, elegant reds: oh, no. This variety makes big, boisterous, joyful wines with high alcohol levels, although relatively low tannins. It tastes of sweet, plummy fruit, sometimes with a hint of chocolate and it has a dry but succulent finish. It has been used and abused in the past to make cheap-and-cheerless, disappointingly dilute wine from irrigated, high-yielding vines, but in recent years there's been a movement towards premium Grenache with loads more flavour, body and guts.

Find it in the south of France, in the Languedoc, in the southern Rhône (as a major component of Châteauneuf-du-Pape, see page 226) and all along the French coast of the Med. It is often blended with Syrah and Mourvèdre. Some Australians take it seriously, particularly Charles Melton in the Barossa Valley, and the Californians are starting to show interest. But the most important country after France for this grape is Spain, where, as Garnacha, it is making increasingly serious and concentrated, powerful reds, usually from old vines. The scenic mountain region of Priorato is the place to go for the serious

monsters, although Tarragona comes a close second. Expect massive wines which may need years to open up. Alvaro Palacios, Clos Erasmus and Clos Mogador are some of the wineries you should look out for.

NEBBIOLO

Nebbiolo is the grape behind Italy's huge Piedmont reds, Barolo and Barbaresco. It ripens late in the autumn, in the mist-covered hills of the region (hence the name Nebbiolo, which means 'foggy'), and it makes a dense wine with high levels of acid and tannin. There's nothing else quite like Nebbiolo, which has a savoury yet floral perfume (some spot roses) and hints of truffles, blackberry and liquorice. Many consider it to be a truly great variety. Certainly, top examples are impressive, refreshingly different and they also age brilliantly. Nebbiolo is hardly ever made elsewhere, partly because mastering its high acidity and thick tannin, while prising some fruity character out, is so difficult. Aldo Conterno, Gaja, Roberto Voerzio and Giacosa are all Italian masters. Prices for the well-known producers are high and you need to beware any really poor vintages. Another hefty Italian that is worth a try is Amarone from Valpolicella, made from the juice of dried grapes (mostly Corvina). It is gloriously thick, ripe and alcoholic and makes a great accompaniment to cheese.

MALBEC

Argentina's greatest success to date has been with the Malbec grape, which originally comes from Cahors but has become a minor vine in France. Immigrants planted it long ago in the Mendoza region and today it produces beautifully rich but rounded, smooth reds packed with black-cherry fruit. It goes brilliantly with steak, and quality is high from many producers.

TANNAT

Uruguay's ace card, according to its fans. Tannat is a thick-skinned, sturdy grape, producing leathery, highly tannic wines with mulberry fruit and toffee-rich depths. Uruguay is fairly unknown to most wine-drinkers, but as more of its producers start to export, look out for Tannat, which does well in the damp maritime climate of this South American country. Not all bottles please – there are too many over-chewy, tannic, thick-set examples – but it can be deliciously different. Tannat's original home is Madiran in southern France, where it again makes very tannic, almost black wine, which will appeal to lovers of rich reds, but which need at least a decade in bottle before they start to open up.

BAGA AND TOURIGA NACIONAL

Two Portuguese varieties capable of making the most interesting and complex reds in the country. Baga is found mainly in Bairrada in northern Portugal. It is a tough grape with a thick skin producing (you guessed it) tannic, powerful wines. In the past, many of these were too heavy-going, but modern vinification methods are now turning up Bairrada reds with softer blackberry and liquorice flavours. Try Luis Pato's wines.

Touriga Nacional, found in port country, is perhaps the most hallowed of all the port grapes. Today it is the mainstay of the Dão region and the new, often brilliant, unfortified red wines coming out of the Douro Valley, the best of which are bursting with intense red fruit and blackcurrant flavours, and have plenty of rounded but firm structure. These wines age well. Good examples are Quinta de la Rosa and Quinta do Crasto, among others. Tip: If you like rich, robust Portuguese red wines, then sip some decent red port from time to time – it's a fortified style (with spirit added) but should appeal hugely.

PINOTAGE

A South African grape developed by crossing Pinot Noir and Cinsault. There used to be a spooky amount of rough, sour, tomatoey Pinotage knocking around, but quality has improved dramatically as Cape winemakers get on top of modern methods, and many more ripe, plummy, carefully oaked wines are now appearing. Cheap Pinotage can be simple stuff, fruity and medium-bodied, but top examples are concentrated, creamily rich and very satisfying. Kanonkop is the most famous producer, but try Longridge, Beyerskloof, Simonsig and Warwick Estate, too. Great with barbecued red meats – so light the braii!

ZINFANDEL

Californian wine can get rather boring with its flood of predictably oaky, rich Chardonnays and Cabernets, so here's a welcome and refreshing change. Zinfandel ('Zin') is a West Coast speciality capable of making generously fruity, full-bodied, often highly alcoholic, reds with a thick, sweetly ripe, raspberry flavour and a twist of black pepper. Most believe that it is the same grape as Italy's Primitivo and was brought over by Italian immigrants. Watch out for a few overblown, over-oaky monsters, but always avoid bland pink and off-white Zin in favour of red. Best producers: Ridge, Seghesio, Frog's Leap and Fetzer Bonterra.

SOUTHERN FRENCH REDS

Do taste some of the richer, peppery styles made in the deep south of France, as well. These include the finer, more serious examples of Corbières, Fitou, Minervois, or reds from Cahors, made from several grapes, including Carignan, Syrah, Mourvèdre, Malbec and Cinsault.

MAKING THE DIFFERENCE

THE FULL-BODIED, ALMOST MOUTH-COATING TEXTURE OF THE WORLD'S BIGGEST REDS COMES FROM TANNIN, WHICH IS A SUBSTANCE FOUND IN THE SKINS, PIPS AND STALKS OF GRAPES. Tannins are a group of complex organic substances also found in bark and other fruits. Tannin from pips is bitter, so canny winemakers take care to avoid crushing the seeds. Some avoid using stems in the mix as well, although others think they benefit the finished wine. The skins provide more benevolent tannins and plenty of colour, too. Powerful reds are made from small berries with thick skins so their concentration of tannin and colour is higher than average. The grapes must be ripe, or a nasty, furry, green tannic character is the result. Extra tannin is added when a wine is aged in new-oak barrels, which leach some of their wood character into the wine.

MATCHING FULL-BODIED REDS WITH FOOD

DON'T SERVE THESE WINES ON THEIR OWN AS THEY ARE TOO HEAVY, and don't even think about matching them with light salads, fish or seafood (salted cod is the only exception), cold chicken, mild cheeses… the wines will walk all over the food and you will hardly taste your dinner. Instead, find a dish that is hearty enough to match your blockbuster wine. Roast red meats, rich stews, peppery steaks, full-flavoured cheeses and hot cheesy bakes are all good candidates. More specifically, match decent Médoc with roast lamb (the mint and blackcurrant of Cabernet complement lamb perfectly), Argentinian Malbec with steak (a modern classic in Buenos Aires), Syrah/Shiraz with game birds or beef casseroles, Barolo and Amarone with fine hard cheeses, Zinfandel with classic Christmas turkey and trimmings, and Pinotage with char-grilled barbecued meats.

STORING AND SERVING

AVOID COMMITTING INFANTICIDE! TOO MANY DRINKERS BUY A FULL-BODIED RED AND CRACK IT OPEN WHEN IT IS FAR TOO YOUNG, ENDING UP WITH A TOUGH, CHEWY WINE IN THEIR GLASS INSTEAD OF A MATURE, MELLOW MOUTHFUL. Beware youthful claret, Barolo and Barbaresco, top Rhône reds and the most serious Australian reds in particular. They will age well for years, if not decades. Store them on their sides in a cool, dark place and leave them well alone. Cheaper wines tend to be made for earlier drinking: within a year or two of purchase. Serve them at room temperature and decant any very heavy reds, just like port, to open up their aroma, soften their texture and possibly remove any solid dregs that lurk at the bottom of the bottle.

FIRST TASTE

Many of these wines can be described as fruity, but this certainly doesn't spell out the whole picture. MANY FULL-BODIED REDS ARE SPICY – BLACK PEPPER, CLOVES, CINNAMON AND NUTMEG – with whiffs of chocolate, cream and toffee, even liquorice and tar, savoury notes and herbs. Cabernet can be minty!

TANNIC REDS NEED FOOD – on their own the structure may seem a little too firm and chewy. The same wine with a steak may seem more balanced as it will work well with the rich protein in the food.

That said, SOME RICH REDS ARE OUT OF BALANCE, steak or no steak. Beware over-tannic reds smelling of freshly planed wood and tasting like chewing on tea bags. Ditch them for subtler wines with more poise.

TASTE THESE WINES AT ROOM TEMPERATURE, not cellar-cold and never fireside-warm.

Open them up way before tasting to let the wine breathe – however, THE MORE EFFECTIVE WAY TO GET A TOUGH RED TO SOFTEN AND MELLOW IS TO DECANT IT before drinking. And swirl it around in big glasses to release its aroma.

BUYER'S GUIDE

■ Good news! THERE ARE PLENTY OF RELIABLE, WELL-PRICED FULL-BODIED REDS out there, including Chilean Cabernet, Australian Cabernet and Cabernet-Shiraz blends…Not dirt-cheap, perhaps, but with loads of food-friendly flavour and concentration for relatively little outlay.

■ VERY CHEAP HEFTY REDS ARE WORTH AVOIDING. Bargain reds, even those made from Shiraz and Cabernet, almost certainly won't deliver a big personality, and may be dilute, bland or jammy.

■ And TREAD MORE CAREFULLY WITH CLARET (RED BORDEAUX) AT LOWER PRICES. It only starts to get reliable in the mid-price range and over, and you still need to be sure to pick a good year, a reputable producer, a fine wine merchant…

■ The top clarets, finest Aussie Shirazes and Italian Barolos all need time, so stash them away for several years or they are a waste of money. DON'T CRACK OPEN EXPENSIVE, RICH REDS UNLESS YOU KNOW THEY WILL BE READY TO DRINK. Use a specialist wine merchant and take advice on individual fine wine purchases.

MOVING ON

■ Once you've sampled one hundred per cent Cabernet and Shiraz, TRY THE BLENDS – most red Bordeaux, Australian Cab-Shiraz, Cabernet-Merlot from around the world – for different flavours, aromas and textures.

■ TRY WINES FROM AS MANY DIFFERENT PARTS OF THE RHÔNE VALLEY AS YOU CAN FIND – this is a fascinating, multi-faceted region with a wide variety of Syrah- and Grenache-based wines. Then head down to the south of France for some more big reds.

■ SET UP A COMPARATIVE TASTING OF OTHER GUTSY REDS – Zinfandel from California, Pinotage from South Africa, Malbec and Tannat from South America.

■ See how full-bodied reds start to lose their tannic grip and soften with age. Some wines, like Barolo or fine claret, are fascinating to watch in development. BUY A FEW BOTTLES OF THE SAME WINE AND OPEN ONE EVERY SIX MONTHS OR SO to track its evolution.

■ EXPERIMENT WITH MATCHING DISHES TO BIG REDS, as these are very food-friendly wines. Try red meat with young claret and game with older versions. Match peppery Syrah with slightly spicy dishes, and decide which is best with mature cheese or roast lamb.

THINK PINK. ROSÉ IS BACK IN VOGUE, AFTER A PERIOD OF BEING SEVERELY UNDERRATED. Nothing compares to a frosty-cold glass of fresh, cerise-coloured wine on a summer's day. Now more and more people are turned on to its charms – men as well as girls! Nonetheless, there are still a few sugary, bland, old-fashioned rosés out there, so it pays to know which ones to select.

Rosé can be made in three ways: red grapes are crushed and the skins left in with the juice for several hours until the colour and flavours have leached into the liquid, which is then fermented; or, for a lighter style, the juice is run off the skins straightaway and fermented; or, occasionally, red wine is blended with white. Because rosé is a fragile wine not built with the structure to last well, you may come across a lot of pink that is past its best and tastes dull and flat. The clever wine-buyer avoids the fading blooms, coming up rosé with the snappiest, most refreshing pinks around. Even when you know how to spot a decent rosé, it's essential to be aware that many different styles of pink wine are made around the world. A fine, delicate rosé from the cool Loire in France is nothing like a rich, powerful Grenache rosé from South Australia. And dryness/sweetness levels vary, too, so be prepared for that. Then it's essential to choose the right moment to sink some pink; perhaps more so than with any other style of wine, rosé only suits certain occasions.

Summery weather, outside dining, light salads and cold meats, fruit and mild cheeses... all these shout 'rosé!'. I never, ever want pink wine in the deep mid-winter, or with a hearty stew, or when I'm drinking by the fireside. That's probably why we all enjoy rosé on our summer holidays but rarely get a kick out of the bottle we bring home and crack open in chilly October! So, pick a pink with care, and pick the perfect

TEXTURE

The lightest rosés are thin and lean, even dilute, but the richest are weighty, almost syrupy in richness.

APPEARANCE

Rosé wine can be anything from almost white, with the very palest tinge of pink, to a bright, sunset peachy-orange, and even a deep cerise, like a light red.

AROMA

Think of red berries – rosé should always have an appealing, fresh fragrance of raspberries, cherries, strawberries or cranberries. Some have more blackcurrant and plums on the bouquet; others smell of rosehip cordial. Look out for a subtle hint of grass on leaner styles and even a whiff of vanilla ice cream – raspberry ripple is quite common!

FLAVOUR

Those red berries should charge through on the palate, too, along with a creaminess on the richer styles. Some rosés have a thin, disappointingly short finish, while the chunkiest have a much more lingering flavour, like a red wine, with some slight tannin on the finish. There should always be a sense of fresh, crisp acidity in rosé. Be aware that while some are bone-dry, others are medium to sweet.

FRANCE

FROM DELICATE TO RIPE

French rosé is still pretty popular, from the delicate pinks of the Loire Valley, to the well-balanced, fruity ones of Bordeaux, and the gutsy, rich wines of the south. Roughly speaking, the further south you head, and the warmer the vineyards become, the richer and riper the rosé gets. Across the land, though, the quality of this wine varies a lot, so choose a French rosé very carefully. Pick a good pink and you'll believe France is the master of this style, but choose a dud and you'll never bother again. Which would be a shame.

LOIRE

Let's start in the Loire Valley in north-central France, where the cool vineyards produce pink wines more delicate, crisp and mouth-watering than those made further south. Unfortunately, this is where you are most likely to come unstuck, as the Loire, a large area with lots of subregions, churns out a wide range of rosé from delicious to dire.

The pale Rosé d'Anjou can be refreshing, if simple in an off-dry style. Made in the area just east of the town of Ancenis, it comes from the rather uninspiring Grolleau grape, which was never destined to make great wine. Rosé d'Anjou is widely available and it is cheap, but there are more exciting pink wines.

Take Cabernet d'Anjou, for example, which is made from a superior grape variety: Cabernet Franc. Like Rosé d'Anjou, it is usually off-dry, but the sweetness is matched by riper, juicier fruitiness, and the quality overall is higher. In the Loire itself, Cabernet d'Anjou is taken more seriously than other rosés. It may be harder to track down, but do try it if you get the chance. Then there's Rosé de Loire, made in Touraine and Anjou-Saumur from Cabernet Franc and sometimes other Loire grapes. This will appeal more to lovers of dry, lip-smacking, thirst-quenching styles of pink.

And finally, the Vins de Pays du Jardin de la France (country wines from the Loire) provide some (usually) decent pink in the form of Cabernet Rosé, which is pleasingly light, dry and tangy, if simple.

BORDEAUX
Further southwest, in Bordeaux, the rosé (just like the white wine) has improved in recent years and now provides some of the most appealing pink around. The majority of Bordeaux rosés are made from Merlot, so you can expect some of that attractive fruity character so typical of this grape, plus (in the best wines) an attractive aroma and a crisp, succulent finish. A typical flavour is fresh strawberries with a dab of cream. A few wines have a little Cabernet Sauvignon and Cabernet Franc in the mix – here, as anywhere, rosé producers make the most of any red grapes going. Bordeaux rosé is well worth trying. As usual with rosé, make sure to crack open a young wine. Top of any rosé-lover's list is the pink from Château de Sours.

PROVENCE
In the deeper south of France, Provence is the source of riper, deeply coloured rosés made mainly from Grenache and Cinsault – these wines can have a juicy rosehip and slightly toffeed character. Some arrive in traditional bottles, shaped like a bowling skittle, with a wide-hipped look to them. A fine Provence rosé is delightful and rich enough to stand up to cold meats and even Mediterranean garlic and tomato dishes, but be aware that there are lots of substandard, oxidised wines around.

REST OF FRANCE
Although plenty of basic table rosé is made in other parts of France, much of it is not exported but simply made to be enjoyed, while young and fresh, in local bars and restaurants.

Pink wines from the Charentes region are a case in point – drunk by the bucketful along the Atlantic coast to wash down moules frites, they are hardly ever seen outside their region. However, another couple of French pinks sometimes encountered overseas are those of Tavel and Lirac in the southern Rhône Valley; these are fairly serious, chunky rosés made from the Rhône red grapes Syrah and Grenache. They taste as though they are packed with ripe red berries, perhaps with a note of spice and caramel. Good stuff. Finally, you may come across Rosé de Riceys, a rare but delicious, still, pink wine made in the Champagne region from the Pinot Noir grape. It has the aroma and flavour of fresh raspberries.

French rosés have their detractors, and I would be the first to agree that quality is alarmingly patchy. But find a decent source of fine French rosé and you'll see why some people love it so much. Many of these discover a favourite local producer while on holiday there, and I'd certainly recommend tasting rosé at the cellar door, as this is where pink wine should be at its most youthful and fresh. Even the simplest, cheapest French rosé can be a delight at such moments. But wherever you are in France, do avoid the ultra-bargain plastic buckets for rosé on sale at the local supermarché as these often taste tired and horrid.

SPAIN

TEMPTING, TANGY ROSADO

I reckon more people have been converted to rosé (or rosado, as it is called here) by drinking Spanish versions than any other. There's something about a chilled, tangy glass of rosado, enjoyed with jamón or prawns by the seaside in Spain that makes us go potty for this style of wine. As usual, we tend to bring the wine home and forget to drink it until it is old and faded, so if you enjoy Spanish rosado in situ, make sure you buy fresh, youthful bottles of it at home, too.

RIOJA AND NAVARRA

Rosado is made in a number of regions from a range of varieties, but the best come from the Rioja and Navarra regions, usually made from either the Tempranillo or Grenache grape (called Garnacha in Spain). Expect the wine to be perfumed and cherryish, dry and mouth-watering – try Chivite's rosado from Navarra for a fine glassful.

REST OF SPAIN

Once you've tried wines from these well-known winemaking areas, go for a modern rosado from Somontano or a rich one from Priorato to ring the changes. And try the local Spanish Bobal grape which can make moreish rosado in Alicante and Utiel-Requena. Valencia's widely seen, inexpensive rosados are pleasantly fruity and moreish when young.

OTHER EUROPEAN ROSÉS

PINK GEMS FROM
THE OLD WORLD

PORTUGAL

Portugal became famous (or should that be infamous?) for rosé with the seventies success story Mateus Rosé. The brand still exists, but nowadays the slightly off-dry, spritzy and pale pink isn't as popular as it used to be. Apart from Mateus, there are few other Portuguese rosés, although the odd one, dry and bright, from the Bairrada region makes an appearance.

ITALY

Italy produces a handful of palatable rosés – or rosatos, as they are known. As in France, the cooler areas, especially the northeast, make crisp, pale, lighter styles, while the warmer south is responsible for richer wines. The fruity, deep-pink Cirò from Calabria, made from the local Gaglioppo grape, is one to sample.

EASTERN EUROPE

The occasional pink gem pops up from this region, although watch out, as standards are patchy, particularly from Bulgaria. Hungary is a better bet, making some clean, crisp and very dry cheapies.

OTHERS FROM EUROPE

It may surprise you to learn that England makes a handful of decent rosés, from a clutch of different grape varieties. The required crispness and freshness is usually there, owing to our cool climate, although some are distinctly sweeter than others. Greece is another unexpected source of modern rosé, with one or two labels making it on to our shelves in recent years. These are mainly produced from local grape varieties and are rather tasty and ripe.

USA

FROM BLUSHING TO GUTSY

There's a type of pink wine made in the US which, strictly speaking, isn't. Pink, that is. It's more a pallid off-white with a faint hint of blush if you hold it up to the light. The aromas are neutral and the flavours are equally disappointing.

CALIFORNIA

Often sweetish, and distinctly lacking in fruit flavours, these 'blush' wines are popular over there, and to a certain extent, over here, too. They are often made from the Zinfandel grape, another cause for complaint, as 'Zin' can be wonderful when made into a hearty red wine, but is decidedly disappointing when forced into producing these weak, bland semi-rosés. 'White Zinfandel', blush

Zinfandel and other lookalikes are widely available on the export market, and, for some people, the sweetness and blandness will be a plus, but do be aware that there are much more exciting rosé wines out there!

Even from California. You see, some of the better West Coast winemakers have now decided to make much riper, deeply coloured rosés, and these wines (in my view, anyway) knock those pale blush rosés for six. Sometimes made from Syrah, occasionally from Grenache, they are pretty gutsy and rich. Try Fetzer's Syrah Rosé as a prime example of new-wave Californian pink wine or one from Bonny Doon's range.

AUSTRALIA

RICH, VIBRANT AND STRONG

Anyone who hates pale and uninteresting rosé should take note – the Aussies make wonderfully rich, vibrant, alcoholic, no-nonsense rosé that is certainly not for wimps!

SOUTH AUSTRALIA

OK, so there aren't exactly hundreds of examples around, but a wine such as Charles Melton's Rosé of Virginia, a cerise-coloured, weighty mouthful of strawberry and cranberry, with a creamy finish, proves the point very well. This wine is made from Grenache in the warm Barossa Valley in South Australia. Geoff Merrill, also working in South Australia, makes another strong, robust rosé.

OTHER REGIONS

You'll find a (very) few rosés in most of the other wine-producing areas of Australia, but look out for the slightly crisper style emerging from cooler spots like the Yarra Vally in Victoria and Tasmania. Hardly any of these make it on to the export market though.

The big, buxom style of Aussie rosé will age for longer than weedier pinks – a good year or so in the case of Melton's wine. The best time to bring out these bottles (and this goes for other very ripe New World styles of pink too) is at a barbie, when they make a great match for prawns, salmon steaks and grilled vegetable kebabs.

ROSÉS FROM THE REST OF THE WORLD

WORTHWHILE PINK GEMS

CHILE AND ARGENTINA

These countries are not well-known for rosé, but a few tasty examples come out of both. Chile produces mainly Merlot- or Cabernet Sauvignon-based rosés, usually fresh and aromatic, while some wineries around the Argentinian winemaking capital of Mendoza turn out sprightly, fruity Syrah-based pinks. South American rosé can be good value for money. Try Miguel Torres' inexpensive example from Chile in the first instance.

REST OF THE WORLD

New Zealand makes one or two worthwhile rosés, particularly in the Marlborough region of the South Island, where the wines taste light, lean and a little grassy. Merlot is usually used. Another part of the world more important for rosé, although perhaps less well-known, is North Africa. Several North African countries produce them from the Southern French grapes Grenache, Syrah and Cinsault. Morocco is the best source: the wines can be more than palatable.

MATCHING ROSÉ WITH FOOD

DECENT ROSÉ IS DELECTABLE ON ITS OWN: TRULY REFRESHING, MOUTH-TINGLING, VIBRANTLY FRUITY WINE FOR A HOT SUMMER'S DAY. It also partners food well, but choose carefully as very rich food will overpower its delicate flavours. A mild goat's cheese salad, a plate of cold ham (jamón), fresh seafood (especially prawns) and pasta with a creamy sauce all make great matches. Very cold, off-dry pink is fairly good at washing down lightly spicy dishes – vegetable samosas spring to mind.

STORING AND SERVING

ROSÉ SHOULD BE CONSUMED WHILE IT IS FRESH AND YOUNG, AS IT SOON LOSES ITS INVITING AROMA AND FLAVOUR. Make sure to buy the youngest vintage you can find and never get palmed off with an elderly bottle of rosé. There's no point in cellaring rosé – drink it up soon after purchase and, once opened, keep it in the fridge and finish it within a day or two. The exceptions are the heartiest, blockbuster Aussie rosés, which may last up to a year.

FIRST TASTE

■ Be aware that ROSÉ IS A FRAGILE WINE and loses its fruity flavours sooner than most. Always buy and drink it up soon after bottling – and once opened, don't leave rosé hanging around. Either finish it within twenty-four hours or ditch it!

■ Pick your moment to crack open a bottle as ROSÉ SUITS HOT-WEATHER DRINKING, either with no food at all, or with light snacks and salads. This is not a wine to drink with rich, hearty dishes.

■ ALWAYS SERVE ROSÉ WELL-CHILLED – even colder than you might serve rich white wines, as the chill emphasises the refreshing, tangy nature of the wine. Frosty glasses of icy rosé always look appealing.

■ If you ever get the chance, ENJOY ROSÉ WHEN TRAVELLING in the wine region itself – it will taste all the more lively and vibrantly fruity for being young and fresh.

BUYER'S GUIDE

■ Although Rosé d'Anjou from the Loire Valley, France, is one of the most commonly seen rosés, it is not always the best – TRY OTHER FRENCH PINKS, especially Bordeaux rosé, and, if you see it, rosé from Tavel or Lirac in the Rhône Valley.

■ They are usually a little more expensive than European ones, but AUSTRALIAN ROSÉS ARE RICHER AND HEARTIER, and the top ones are serious bottles that would go down well at a barbie.

■ Always, always, BUY THE YOUNGEST ROSÉ YOU CAN FIND either in the shops or off a wine list. Aim for a very recent vintage. Reject anything too old or your pink will have lost its bloom.

■ Taste even the very cheapest rosés if you get the chance because THERE ARE A FEW GENUINE BARGAINS out there. It's well worth sampling a few different labels of inexpensive rosé at the start of summer and picking the one you like best for future buying.

MOVING ON

■ FOR PARTY PINKS, TRY CHILEAN OR ARGENTINIAN ROSÉS. There aren't too many around, but they are good value and make a change from French or Spanish ones.

■ Move on from boring basic Californian 'blush' and TRADE UP TO THE NEW-WAVE, GUTSY WEST COAST ROSÉS with bags more colour and flavour.

■ TRY MOROCCAN ROSÉ, which is surprisingly tasty from a country not exactly renowned for its winemaking prowess!

■ EXPERIMENT BY MATCHING ROSÉS WITH A WIDE RANGE OF DISHES, such as mildly spicy food, cold meats, barbecues, buffet fare – you'll be surprised at how many exciting partners you find.

PART THREE

WINE
KNOW-HOW.

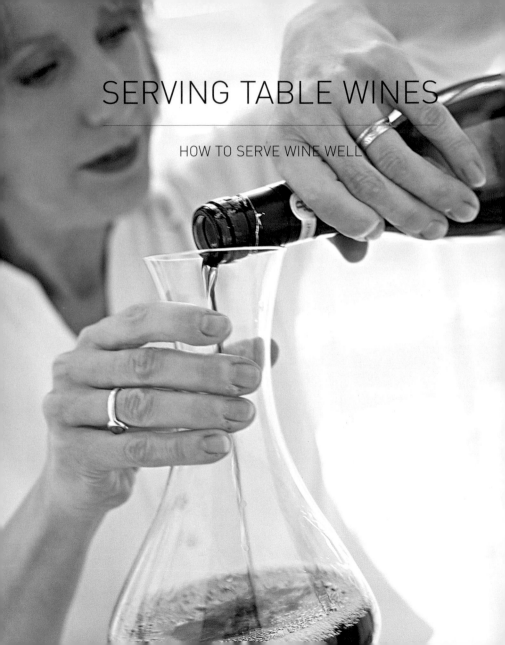

SERVING TABLE WINES

HOW TO SERVE WINE WELL

Here's how to serve wine well. Uncork the wine and remove any bits of cork crumble from around the lip of the bottle (they won't affect the flavour but look bad in a glass). Then slowly pour the wine into the glass, filling it only one-third of the way up. This doesn't mean you are stingy, but it lets you swirl the liquid around, and savour its appearance and aroma. Do what the experts do – fill it up frequently, but never to the top (unless it's a Champagne flute, which looks odd half-empty). This is helpful for keeping whites cold, too, as it means the wine stays in the bottle in a cool spot, rather than warming up in your glass.

Pour rich reds, especially older ones, with care. They may have a sediment that has collected in the bottom of the bottle over the years (or along its side if it has been in a rack). No one wants to sip a mouthful of black gunk, so remove the sediment by decanting the bottle gradually into a glass decanter (or a clean jug). Stop when the sediment starts to appear in the liquid. Chuck away the dregs.

It's also worth decanting rich, tannic reds, which don't have a sediment, as exposure to the air mellows them, allowing their aroma and flavour to emerge. Forget about opening the bottle half an hour before dinner; it won't have a great effect on the liquid. Instead, decant the wine into another container or serve in big-bowled glasses to aerate it.

The ideal wineglass is neither a pricey crystal one nor a modern, coloured one. To see your wine properly, go for plain glass, and choose a thin one, as that feels much nicer on the mouth than chunky, thick glass does. Pick glasses with long stems, so you can hold them there, rather than wrapping your fingers round the bowl, warming up the wine. And go for a fairly big bowl so you can swirl the wine and release its aroma.

DETECTING FAULTS IN WINE

It doesn't pay to be a wimp if you think your wine is faulty. Many of us are embarrassed about complaining, when we are quite comfortable to make a fuss about poor food, bad clothes or rip-off holidays. I'll let you in on a secret that some of the wine trade want to keep hidden: there's no special mystery about faulty wine.

If you don't like a wine, take it back to the shop, or send it back if you're in a restaurant. You do not have to understand the problem like a top-ranking merchant does. Just explain that the wine tastes of vinegar, or smells musty, or looks cloudy or so on. As long as you haven't drained the bottle (that would be taking the mick) you can expect to receive a replacement – a new bottle of the same wine or a similarly priced one.

There is one proviso when returning wine, however: try not to complain that the wine is not the style you like. There's a big difference between a faulty wine and one that doesn't suit you. A kind retailer might replace a wine bought in error, but not everyone will. Restaurants are especially snooty about this.

If you keep buying the wrong sort of wine, make sure you ask more questions about a bottle before you buy it, or read this book carefully before you go shopping. You can't expect to take back an extremely cheap white, say, just because it is a bit boring, or a bargain-basement red because it is a touch over-oaky. No, we're talking faults here: nasty, bitter, acidic, over-sweet, mouldy, flabby, oxidised wine. No one should shell out good money for something that tastes truly revolting!

The most prevalent wine fault is caused by cork taint. Corked wine has nothing to do with a crumbling cork. It means a mould-affected cork has spoilt the wine, giving a musty aroma and cardboard flavour (think damp cardboard, old kitchen clothes, even mushrooms). This trait can be quite pronounced in some wines, but disarmingly subtle in others, sometimes just deadening the fresh-fruit aroma and taste of the wine. Corked wine gets worse the longer it is opened, so if you're not sure, wait awhile and try it again. If you suspect the wine is corked (you can't prove it and shouldn't have to), take or send it back, and demand a replacement. Despite some efforts on the part of the cork industry, the number of corked bottles remains unacceptably high – some estimates put it as one in eight bottles. This is the main reason why plastic corks and screwcaps are sometimes used instead. Use of screwcaps for premium wines, especially in New Zealand and Australia, is on the rise.

Other faults to look out for include oxidised wine (where air has got in and spoilt it), wine with 'foreign objects' in it (I found tiny fruit flies on one memorable occasion), and heavily sulphured wine. Sulphur is used as a preservative when most wines are bottled, but overuse leads to a wine which smells of struck matches, and this may cause problems to asthma sufferers and others allergic to this chemical. The stricter regulations for organic wine mean it usually contains less sulphur. Send stinking sulphurous wines back!

Don't worry about wine that has thrown a natural sediment (see page 277) or ones with little white crystals in the bottle. The latter are harmless tartrate deposits which won't affect the taste of your wine.

STORING WINE

DO YOU NEED A SERIOUS STORAGE PLAN?

You don't need a serious storage plan to keep bottles for a week or two, obviously, but do think about where and how you store them if they are hanging around for longer. Keep wines in a cool, dark spot as this fragile liquid suffers in the heat (or, worse, where temperatures fluctuate). I'm especially bothered by mini wine racks near the oven. The kitchen is not ideal for wine as it gets much too hot, nearly every day. Wine stored in sunny places quickly loses its fresh fruitiness, so don't leave it on the windowsill in summer, either!

MAKESHIFT CELLARS

There are plenty of places in the home where wine can be kept. The cupboard under the stairs is a good bet – make sure you don't store any white spirits or pungent paints there as well, since there's some evidence that wine can be affected by strong-smelling substances. Lay bottles on their sides. This stops the cork from drying out – a shrivelled-up cork can let air in and spoil the wine. If you invest in a small wine rack, go for a wooden one – metal ones can tear the labels. Alternative spots include: the bottom of a wardrobe, under the spare bed... anywhere, really, where it stays relatively cool and dark and where you are not likely to disturb your bottles. The garage is not a great idea, as it can get very cold, and often has petrol or paint fumes. Some people worry about leaving white and sparkling wines in the fridge for any length of time. There's nothing wrong with storing everyday bottles in there for a day or two, but be sure it isn't too cold when you serve it – a serious chill can mute flavour and aroma.

PROFESSIONAL WINE STORAGE

If you want to start a serious collection then a cellar is the best storage option; it tends to be cooler, darker and sometimes a little humid: perfect conditions for wine. Empty it of all smelly substances, but don't repaint it or wash it down with lots of cleaning fluid – wine doesn't mind dirt but may be affected by chemicals in the air. Line a wall or two with decent racks and buy some cellar tags to help you identify bottles. It's possible to keep wine in its original case, as well as on a rack; as long as the bottles are lying on their sides and can't break, they'll be fine. It may be worth keeping a 'cellar book' to record when you opened the wine and what it tasted like – especially if you have lots of the same bottles, as you can chart its development.

OTHER OPTIONS

Wine buffs who lack cellars can still build an impressive collection. One option is a temperature-controlled unit that looks like a fridge, but is filled with racks and designed to keep wines in exactly the right conditions. These are expensive (expect to splash out at least £800) but may be worth the investment. Pricier still are spiral-shaped cellars that are bored into the ground floor of your home. These cost nearer £5,000– £10,000 but are impressive: a small circular underground cellar is created, lined with racks and a central staircase to provide access. It may even add value onto your home. Most of us find a solution to the problem. I know a Londoner who keeps his loot in the outside loo with a thermostat to control the temperature. Others keep theirs with a wine storage specialist.

WINES WORTH HANGING ON TO

As a rule of thumb, the lighter and less substantial the wine (think Pinot Grigio, Muscadet, basic Beaujolais, cheap fizz), the more quickly you must open it. Richer 'everyday' wines (non-European Chardonnay, Cab-Shiraz blends, ordinary Rhône reds) last a bit longer unopened – up to a year after purchase – before starting to lose their vibrant flavours and aromas. Note that red Rioja, even a very expensive label, is aged at the winery in Spain and released ready to drink. Likewise LBV (late-bottled vintage) and tawny ports. Don't be tempted to store them for long.

But some wines are supposed to be kept – actually tasting better if you lay them down for a period. Among these are young, tough premium reds from Bordeaux (claret); rich, tannic Cabernets and Cabernet blends from the southern hemisphere; vintage Champagnes; fine German Rieslings, both sweet and dry (and similar bottles from Austria); top Australian Semillons; top-of-the-range Rhône reds; Barbarescos, Amarones and Barolos from Italy; and best Loire Valley whites. These all benefit from some bottle-age (assuming you buy recent vintages), becoming more mellow, their acidity softer, their flavours more well-knit, with honeyed undertones in the whites and earthier, smoother, gamey notes in the reds.

It's obviously a matter of taste whether you prefer mature or youthful wines. In the case of certain styles, like red burgundy, there is something to be said for the bright, red-fruit character of the younger wines and the truffley, horsey, richly gamey character of older ones. As with so many things in the world of wine, work out which suits you best. A serious collection should give you ample opportunity to try out wines both young and old!

HOW TO TASTE WINE

DON'T SKIP THIS IF YOU ASSUME TASTING WINE LIKE A PRO MEANS LOOKING LIKE AN IDIOT! Okay, it might do, but taking your time to think about this precious liquid will definitely help you learn an enormous amount about it. I reckon ninety-nine per cent of all wine slips down our throat without touching the sides, so that while a little of its unique character comes through, not much does. If you look at wine carefully, then smell it properly, and finally take your time tasting it, you should notice a lot of interesting characteristics starting to emerge, for good or bad. Then you will almost certainly enjoy fine wine a great deal more. The best thing about tasting is that no one is 'right' or 'wrong' in deciding what a wine tastes like. It's just a matter of building up points of reference that mean something to the individual taster. If you still think you'll look like an idiot, practise the following steps in the bath, spitting out at your toes – that's what a lot of the experts do – until it feels like second nature!

LOOK

The appearance of any wine can tell you much about the sort of style to expect.

SNIFF

Swirl the liquid to release its aroma –
it's an important part of a wine's appeal.

SLURP

Swoosh the wine around your mouth
to bring out the full flavour. Think
about its taste and texture.

SPIT

The 'finish' of a wine is important.
Consider its richness or lightness,
length of flavour and general appeal.

LOOK

The appearance of wine is important, so really peer at the liquid in your wine glass. It helps if you choose a plain glass, not a cut or coloured one, with a tall stem. Tipping the glass to one side helps, holding it way down the stem, especially when assessing the depth of colour in your red: look at the rim of the liquid, not the middle. A wine should look clear, not cloudy, without bits of sediment floating in it (see page 277). Look at the viscosity of the liquid: a rich, thick wine leaves noticeable trails, or 'legs', down the side of the glass after you have swirled. This can indicate high alcohol levels or sweetness. Red wines with an almost bluish tinge tend to taste younger than those with a brick-red, brownish colour, and those that have turned brown may well be past it. In whites, a deep golden colour indicates a rich wine, which could be oaky or lusciously sweet. A pale-straw hue means a drier, lighter style in your glass.

SNIFF

Now for the aroma. ('Bouquet' is another, somewhat old-fashioned term for describing the aroma; some experts call it the 'nose'.) Swirl the wine around your glass before you smell it, as this releases its aroma. Now stick your nose near the liquid and take a big sniff, or a series of small sniffs. A wine's scent is very important, acting as an introduction to the flavour. This simple test is often overlooked, so linger over it. Does the wine smell appealing or not? Does it seem clean and fresh or sulphurous, vegetal or musty? Is it a subtle smell or a rich, pungent one? Think about the fruit character – citrus fruits, perhaps, or red berries, or bananas. Maybe take it further: what sort of citrus fruits (lemons, oranges, grapefruit...), what sort of berries (raspberries, redcurrants...), fresh bananas or banana sweeties, or even banoffee pie? Look out for vanilla, cream, spice and pepper, too, and other more eclectic nuances.

SLURP

Take a small sip and swirl the liquid around your mouth, even drawing some air through it and swooshing it around to release the full flavour. Look for similar characteristics in the flavour – fruit, cream, spice – but at the same time consider other elements, such as its weight, structure or body and how acidic or refreshing it is. Try to decide whether this is a rich or a light wine, a tart wine, or a heavy, dense or oily one. Is it tannic – tannins produce a furry sensation in the mouth, like sucking on a tea bag – or bone-dry or honeyed and sweet? Think about whether it is simply a big, rich, impressive wine, perhaps one that you might not want to drink in any quantity, but which is simply a show-off in character! Lighter, simpler wines are sometimes more enjoyable or food-friendly. Finally, is the wine well-balanced, or does it have over-the-top tannins, mouth-puckering acidity or is its sweetness out of kilter?

SPIT

Professional wine tasters (almost) always spit wine out to save their sobriety, but they don't stop assessing the wine as they spit. The 'finish' of a wine is the final important factor. Does it leave a lingering flavour or does it disappear from the taste buds in a disappointing way? This provides another opportunity to assess texture: is it a rich, gloopy wine or a thin, light one? Again, look out for those unusual nuances – perhaps black pepper in a Syrah, or chocolate in a Merlot – as these often come through on the finish more than ever. Sometimes wine faults show up on the finish. A corked wine might leave a musty taste in the mouth, while an over-acidic wine may be wincingly tart at the very end. Tannins also tend to show through at this stage more than any other. If your wine leaves a chewy, furry, 'tea-leaf' texture in your mouth, it's tannic and may need time to soften up, or a rare steak to accompany it.

SPECIAL OCCASIONS

You don't need to buy expensive Champagne – in fact, you don't have to have Champagne at all! If you do splash out, go for a reliable name or taste a cheaper Champers in advance.

Beware pricey vintage Champagnes that are not mature (they should be at least six years old). Plenty of non-European sparklers, French crémants and Spanish cavas will go down just as well as inferior Champagnes – often for a fraction of the price.

One idea is to buy a few bottles of fine Champagne for the toasts, and lots of cheaper fizz for the rest of the bash. Consider magnums as well.

If booking a venue where you are required to serve house wines, be sure to taste them well in advance of your event. If they are poor, say so and ask for something different.

Make sure your fizz is *brut* (dry). This is not the moment for a sweet wine like Asti, unless it is specifically to serve with a celebration cake.

Don't be tempted by cut-price wines from a discount warehouse (unless you get a good taste of it first). Trade up from the bargain basement and stick to medium price brackets for something safe and palatable.

Make sure the wines are relatively young and fresh, and be sure to have chilled the whites and sparklers. Ensure the reds are not too jammily hot. Warm wine will taste horrible, especially at an over-crowded event.

Choose easy-drinking, soft, fruity wines – not ones with 'difficult' characteristics. Aim to buy crowd-pleasers that slip down easily, and don't show off with unusual styles.

PACKAGING WINE

The vast majority of wines sold come in 75cl glass bottles. This standard size of bottle is supposed to be perfect for sharing between two, and anyway, if you don't finish it in one sitting, the wine should keep well for a couple of days. That said, I think there are alternatives that could be considered from time to time.

Half-bottles are a grand idea if you only want a glass or two; I would recommend buying these rather than resealing a bigger bottle as wine does start to deteriorate from the moment it is exposed to air. Pick half-bottles if you are trying out new styles of wine, too, that way it won't matter so much if you choose something you don't like. Always buy halves for the wines that tend to be enjoyed at just one particular time of year, but are rejected the rest of the time. Make more of these small bottles.

Sadly, big bottles are equally over-looked. Why don't we buy more magnums (one and a half litres, the equivalent of two ordinary bottles) or even Jereboams (six bottles)? Larger bottles look great at special celebrations, somehow convincing guests that we have been wildly generous when, in fact, an equal volume of wine bought in ordinary bottles usually costs about the same. Magnums are widely available for premium wine as well as for the cheapies like Lambrusco and Liebfraumilch, although an independent wine merchant may be your best bet for tracking down a wide range of serious big bottles. Jereboams are rarer, and the huge Methuselahs (or eight bottles), Balthazars (sixteen bottles) and Nebuchadnezzars (twenty bottles) are even scarcer, and mainly restricted to Champagne.

If you want to buy large-format bottles for laying down in a cellar, bear in mind that the wine tends to age more slowly in them (and conversely more quickly in halves) – it's to do with the proportion of wine exposed to the sides and top of the bottle. Oh, and they won't fit in your usual wine racks, either!

Bottled wine is sealed with a natural cork, a plastic stopper or a screw cap. An unacceptably high number of bottles is spoilt by the pesky mould that can occur when bark is used to plug a bottle. Metal screw caps are slowly coming into vogue and are being used by more quality wine producers than ever before. Although they seem less classy than natural cork, they fulfil their role of sealing wine well and bring no taint into the equation. Plastic stoppers have similar benefits. Plastic and metal screw caps are, however, not biodegradable and there is some debate over whether they allow wine to age well as they let no air in at all. Despite this, until manufacturers of corks sort out their problems, it's my guess wine drinkers will increasingly seek out these alternative 'closures'. After all, you wouldn't buy milk in cartons if one in every twenty pints was spoilt by its packaging, would you? So why put up with cork taint?

Finally, wine boxes are a convenient container for wine if you are having a party and don't feel like opening bottles all night. Generally, they hold three litres of wine. Don't expect serious, sophisticated wine to come in boxes, as more everyday, easy-drinking styles tend to be packaged in this way. I don't recommend boxes if you plan to siphon off just one glass from time to time, as the wine will deteriorate gradually in this type of packaging – or quickly, if a hole or leak develops in the bag. Use when entertaining crowds, and bear in mind some people think they are a bit naff!

TIPS FOR BUYING WINE

Even those with a good knowledge of wine can find it pretty disarming to be faced with rows of bottles in a supermarket or off-licence. It's clearly easier to grab a familiar bottle every time, but as I have made clear throughout this book, that can mean you get stuck in a boring rut, always drinking the same grapes from the same region and even the same producer. The world of wine is so richly endowed with different styles that it would be a shame to get fed up with the liquid in your glass.

So the first and most essential tip to the wine shopper is be prepared to experiment. Make a point of avoiding a bottle that is tried and tested in your house; instead plump for something quite different, be it a new grape variety – how about Viognier, Sémillon, Cabernet Franc? Or a new region: Greece, Uruguay

and Portugal are all fascinating right now. In particular, avoid the very big brands. There may be nothing wrong with them, and they may well represent reasonable quality, reliable wine at a decent price, but *everyone* drinks them and they usually fail to offer much excitement. With smaller producers you are more likely to get a handcrafted, characterful product. And besides, your neighbours won't all have it in their wine racks too.

Think about the various outlets that offer wine and decide which ones work best for you on different occasions. Supermarket wine departments have been thoroughly revolutionised since the late twentieth century and these outlets stock an impressive range of styles and price points. Their turnover is fast, so wines are likely to be fresh, and they can offer worthwhile discounts because of their buying power. Supermarkets are convenient, of course, as you can buy your booze at the same time as your weekly food shop and choose wines that match your cooking easily.

On the other hand, some argue that supermarkets still lack the knowledgeable assistance offered by a specialist merchant. A fine wine merchant is certainly a great place to go if you are searching for something different and might need some help in choosing. Make sure you quiz the assistant hard and perhaps even ask for a taste of wine – independents sometimes have a bottle or two of interesting stuff open to try.

It's worth seeking out a specialist merchant if you are developing a love of a particular type of wine. And there are now a few impressive smaller outlets with a serious emphasis on non-European wines. Don't forget mail order or internet wine buying, too. Make sure that you always use a well-established, reputable company, however.

Look out for 'bin end' offers, which indicates the end of a stock of wine (a few bottles left over that are being sold at a special price). In general, though, be sure to avoid wines that are past it, looking tired and stewing gently on a dusty shelf.

Finally, take a good look at any information you are offered in-store: shelf descriptions or press recommendations (not a fool-proof guide to your own likes and dislikes, but probably a fair indication of the style of wine), labels, leaflets and in-store magazines. We all need as much help as possible when buying wine if we can't actually taste the stuff, so make good use of what is there to help you decide. Above all else, trust your own tastebuds and get sampling as much as possible.

Many thanks to the team at Quadrille, especially Jane, Lisa and Helen, for all their hard work, expertise and enthusiasm. Thanks as well to my agent Martine Carter and Jamie Ambrose for proofreading the original manuscript. Most of all, thanks to my family for putting up with me while this book took shape.